Extending literacy

Children reading and writing non-fiction

David Wray and Maureen Lewis

London and New York

First published 1997
by Routledge
2 Park Square, Milton Park, Abingdon, Oxon, OX14 4RN

Simultaneously published in the USA and Canada
by Routledge
270 Madison Ave, New York NY 10016

Transferred to Digital Printing 2006

Typeset in Times by Solidus (Bristol) Limited

British Library Cataloguing in Publication Data
A catalogue record for this book is available from the British Library

Library of Congress Cataloguing in Publication Data
Wray, David, 1950–
    Extending literacy: children reading and writing
    non-fiction/David Wray and Maureen Lewis.
        p.   cm.
    Includes bibliographical references and index.
    ISBN 0-415-12829-3. – ISBN 0-415-12830-7
    1. Prose literature – Study and teaching. 2. Children – Books and
    reading. 3. English language – Composition and exercises – Study
    and teaching. I. Lewis, Maureen. II. Title.
LB1575.W73   1997
372.64 '044–dc20
                                              96-25697
                                                    CIP

ISBN 0-415-12829-3 (hbk)
ISBN 0-415-12830-7 (pbk)

Publisher's Note
The publisher has gone to great lengths to ensure the quality of this reprint
but points out that some imperfections in the original may be apparent

Printed and bound by CPI Antony Rowe, Eastbourne

Extending lite

There have always been concerns over the standard of children's literacy. This book addresses two particular problems. First, just how well are children's skills extended, once they have mastered the 'basics' of literacy? Second, how effectively do children interact with non-fiction books?

Despite the fact that the majority of adult literacy experiences are with non-fiction texts, narrative is still the dominant genre in children's classroom writing and reading. Furthermore, there is evidence that when children do use non-fiction texts, they often do little more than copy sections from reference books.

This book tackles these issues and shows how teachers can use a range of non-fiction sources to develop the literacy skills of their pupils. It draws extensively upon the findings of the Exeter Extending Literacy (EXEL) project, which was set up specifically to explore ways in which non-fiction might be used more effectively to extend pupils' skills in reading and writing.

The book covers in detail many useful teaching strategies and approaches which have been developed in collaboration with primary school teachers.

David Wray is Reader in Literacy in Education at the University of Exeter, and is a former primary school teacher. He has written and edited over twenty books on language and literacy, including *English 7–11* (Routledge 1995).

Maureen Lewis is Senior Lecturer in Language and Literacy in the Rolle School of Education at the University of Plymouth. She was Research Fellow on the EXEL project and has also worked as a primary school teacher. She has published widely on children's interactions with non-fiction.

Contents

List of figures

Acknowledgements

In September 1992 we began work on the Exeter Extending Literacy (EXEL) Project, based at the University of Exeter School of Education. Thanks to the generous support and funding of the Nuffield Foundation we were able to spend three years developing ways of helping children interact more effectively with non-fiction texts. We were privileged to work with many talented and dedicated teachers and we wish to record our thanks to all of the many teachers and advisors who invited us to work in their classrooms and offered us critical support and many thoughtful insights.

We would especially like to thank the following who invited us to work within their authorities – Ashvin Bhabuta (Hackney), Karen Feeney and Paul Hann (Lewisham), Janice Gravett (Kingston-upon-Thames), Jane Richards and Michael Morgan (Doncaster), Janet Brennan (Devon), Chris Edwards and John Sinker (Cornwall), Sally Lawson and Pamela Weston (Wirral), Daphne Denaro (Isle of Wight), Nikki Daly and Richard Boxall (Tower Hamlets) and Cathy Coulthard (Enfield).

Many individual teachers worked with us and we would especially like to thank Carolyn Ballard, Margaret Birch, Andrea Bradshaw, Clair Brown, Caroline Cox, Rosie Culverhouse, Jenny Earlham, Stuart Earlham, David Edwards, Gary Edwards, Yvonne Etherington, Olive Ferdinand, Roger Grant, Siân Hodgson, Jill Jordan, Sonya Lamoon, Sarah Llamas, Caroline Lorenzi, Jan Marshall, Christa Mitchell, Jane Richards, Sheila Rogers, Patricia Rospigliosi, Chris Stratton, Suzanne Stoddard, Maggie Williams, Linda Whish, Dawn Whittaker and Ian Worthington for their help and for the examples of children's work that are included within this book.

We are also grateful to the editors of the journals *Support for Learning* (National Association for Special Educational Needs) and *Early Years* for kindly agreeing to allow us to use in this book material previously published in their journals.

David Wray and Maureen Lewis
Exeter, April 1996

Chapter 1

Extending literacy
An introduction to the project

SOME BACKGROUND

The early 1990s was characterised by a great deal of media and professional attention being given to the issue of the standards in literacy achieved by primary schools, particularly in reading. While much of this attention was misguided, and indeed often unwelcome, it did, however, almost as a by-product, draw attention once again to the teaching of literacy beyond the basic stages. What teaching were children receiving who had already made a start on the learning of reading and writing? Were these skills being extended in schools, or was it simply assumed that once children had mastered the 'basics' of reading and writing all they then required were merely a range of opportunities to use these?

Concern about this area is not, of course, new. In their 1978 survey of primary schools (DES, 1978) HMI found 'little evidence that more advanced reading skills were being taught' (para. 5.30). Their 1990 report on the teaching of reading in primary schools makes almost the identical statement and suggests that research such as that reported by Southgate, Arnold and Johnson (1981) and by Lunzer and Gardner (1979), for all its headline-making when published, had had little real effect upon teaching practice.

Relating to the teaching of writing, the 1978 HMI report's comments again seemed to predict current issues in their identification of the lack of range of writing set by junior school teachers (para. 5.36) and the extensive use of copying rather than original composition (para. 5.33). Similar issues have been identified by the National Writing Project and work on children's activities in 'project work' (Kerry and Eggleston, 1988). Recent work in Australia, now becoming known in this country (Littlefair, 1991; Martin, 1989), has suggested that much more attention needed to be given to the issue of genre in children's reading and writing, and that there was a body of linguistic knowledge with which teachers needed to familiarise themselves if they were successfully to help children cope with the reading and writing demands of schooling and of the world beyond school.

A more recent HMI report (DES, 1991) highlighted the problems which teachers of children aged seven to eleven seem to have had in preparing themselves for the demands of the United Kingdom National Curriculum for English at Key Stage 2. The inspectors reported that in English 'too many Key Stage 2 teachers remained unaware of how far removed their current practices were from the requirements of the national curriculum and lacked sufficient in-service training to make changes'. These curriculum demands seemed therefore to have set some targets which many schools were finding very difficult to meet.

Because of concerns about issues such as these, members of the Primary Language team at the University of Exeter School of Education embarked upon a linked programme of research into aspects of the teaching of literacy in the junior school (Fox, 1993; Lewis, 1992; Poulson, 1992; Wray and Lewis, 1992) and, from this research and that of others, several problematic areas seemed to emerge. These are detailed below although it should be stressed that this way of reporting suggestions from research is inevitably open to the charge of caricature. There are many junior classrooms to whom the following statements do not apply.

SOME CURRENT PROBLEMS

Problem 1: The limited range and quality of junior school children's interactions with reading material of all kinds

Narrative is very definitely the dominant genre both in children's reading and writing and, where efforts are made to enhance and deepen children's responses to text, these seem to be confined to experiences with narratives of one kind or another. Yet it has been quite forcibly pointed out by Martin (1989), among several others, that the bulk of adult experience with texts involve interactions with genres other than narrative.

Problem 2: The patchy teaching which children receive in using reading as a means of learning across a wide variety of curriculum contexts

For all the exhortations of the Bullock report (DES, 1975) regarding the importance of 'language across the curriculum', it is still rare for teachers to specifically teach children to read in history, geography, science, mathematics, etc. Practice seems rather to involve teaching children to read and then simply providing them with a range of curriculum contexts in which to practise their reading. The effects of this are clearly seen in research findings such as those of the Application of Subject Knowledge project at the University of Exeter which have detailed the very low level of junior children's responses to the texts they are given to read in mathematics and science (Desforges, 1993).

Problem 3: Children's difficulties in handling information, that is, in specifying, locating and effectively using sources of written information, for example in libraries

There has been a long-standing concern about children's acquisition of information skills, variously referred to as library skills, research skills and study skills (Wray, 1985). The most common teacher complaint arising from this concern is usually expressed as 'How can I stop my children copying from reference books?' From the findings of our own research (Wray and Lewis, 1992), it appears that most junior children are quite aware that they should not copy from reference books, and can usually give a cogent set of reasons why not, but when they are actually engaged in the practical tasks of locating and selecting information in books will revert to copying behaviour with little demur.

Problem 4: The difficulties teachers find in assessing children's development in this extended use of literacy

This problem is actually not at all surprising. There has been sufficient controversy about the principles and practices of assessing initial reading for one to guess that a more elaborated notion of literacy will be difficult to assess adequately. It has been suggested (Poulson, 1992) that teachers evolve their own practices in this area which often conflict radically with more established (and, especially, Government-approved) ideas of practice.

UNDERLYING ISSUES

These problem areas seem to stem from two, linked, causes. Firstly, many teachers, particularly of Key Stage 2 children, do not appear to have extensive knowledge about the development of literacy. Many complain that they received little input on these topics either in their initial teacher education or in subsequent in-service work. Whatever the truth of this (and we suspect that it is less true now than it was five years ago), it is certainly the case that it only takes a few discussions with otherwise well-informed junior school teachers to get a sense of their own feelings of inadequacy in the face of even the limited National Curriculum demands for the extension of literacy. Some evidence relating to this point, and arising from our own research, is presented in Chapter 2 of this book.

Secondly, we have not yet identified and practised a sufficient range of effective strategies for the implementation of curriculum changes. As mentioned earlier, the problems identified here are not new. They have been documented for some considerable time and, indeed, sensible research-based suggestions for ways to overcome them have also been made. During the early 1980s a good deal of attention was given to the Lunzer and Gardner

(1979; 1984) idea of DARTs: Directed Activities Relating to Texts. Activities such as cloze procedure, prediction exercises and sequencing texts became popular for a time yet a close observation of actual teaching practice today suggests that such activities have often simply been added to the list of 'reading exercises' which are thought to be 'good' for children. There is little questioning of 'good for what?'

Because of the lack of real depth in teachers' understanding of the development of literacy and the lack of effective curriculum development strategies, it seems that, where developments are taking place, there is a tendency for teachers and schools to rely upon published materials to guide their teaching. This would not necessarily be problematic but, unfortunately, with very few exceptions, published materials produced for the purpose of extending literacy seem to be based around pupil 'exercises' which are decontextualised and therefore make it difficult for teachers to ensure that children apply skills in other, wider situations. If real benefits are to accrue it is particularly important that work with children should stress meaningful and purposeful applications of extended literacy (Wray, 1985).

THE OBJECTIVES OF THE EXEL PROJECT

Responding to the challenge set by the analysis above, in September 1992 we embarked upon a curriculum development project funded by the Nuffield Foundation for an initial two year period (subsequently extended to three years) and known as the Exeter Extending Literacy (EXEL) project. The project had the ultimate aim of producing materials which would assist teachers of junior school children to develop more effectively the literacy of their pupils. It was also anticipated that teachers of children both older and younger than this would find these materials of benefit. The project was founded upon several key ideas which are outlined briefly below.

1   Learning to read and to write are only the first steps in the process of becoming fully literate. They are complemented by the activities of reading and writing to learn. In fact we would argue that it makes little sense to talk about these skills in any kind of hierarchical way and the labelling of these as 'advanced' or 'higher-order' skills has, in fact, been one of the reasons why primary teachers have not made greater strides in their development. From our experience, some of which is documented in later chapters of this book, infant children are quite capable of using literacy as a tool for learning even before they are fully competent in 'the basics'.

2   The use of reading and writing in this way are, by definition, curriculum-wide processes. Reading and writing can never be pigeon-holed as simply 'English' activities and children read and write in virtually all other curriculum areas. This suggests that each curriculum area offers its own

opportunities for the teaching of reading and writing as well as of specific content. Many of the examples of children's work which we present in subsequent chapters of this book come from curriculum areas such as history, geography and science.

3   In their use of reading and writing across the curriculum children can naturally encounter and should be expected to produce a wide range of text types. The kinds of texts which are usually read and written in history, for example, will be different from those in science, or mathematics. This text range is hardly ever considered as an issue by teachers yet can be a crucial element determining children's understanding.

4   These interactions in curriculum contexts should mirror the kinds of interactions children have with texts in the world outside school. The fact is that reading and writing are not things which children only engage in inside the walls of classrooms. Merely to walk along the average town High Street involves anybody, including young children, in considerable exercise of literacy. It seems perverse for teachers to ignore these experiences and treat the activities of reading and writing in completely different ways to their use in the world outside the classroom.

5   These real-life interactions with texts tend to be characterised by several features (Wray, Bloom and Hall, 1989).

- They are purposeful. As adults we scarcely ever read or write without knowing very clearly why we are doing so, yet how often is this true of children's reading and writing in school?
- They demand the use of a range of strategies in the text user: from skimming and scanning to the intensive reading of every word on a page; from rough note-taking to painstaking final draft writing.
- They make reference to and rely upon knowledge of other texts. Most adult texts locate their meanings in a complex web of intertextuality. Advertisements are a good example of this – to understand a particular advertisement for a brand of coffee, the reader/viewer needs to have read/watched previous episodes in the mini soap opera. Good children's books also rely on intertextual knowledge (how could you read Janet and Alan Ahlberg's *Each Peach, Pear, Plum* without already knowing the nursery rhyme characters it uses?) yet often the books children are given to read in school lack this feature (Hynds, 1993).
- They have definite outcomes. Things happen as a result of reading and writing outside school. We read the timetable and catch the train, we complete the form and an appropriate tax code arrives. Children in school, however, are often rather puzzled about what they are reading and writing for and outcomes, if there are any, arrive much later.

6   Children learn to interact critically and purposefully with texts by

engaging in critical and purposeful behaviour; that is, the process is not that of practising the 'skills' of being a critical and effective user of text which they then apply to real texts, but rather one of learning through activities which are authentic in their own rights.

Some materials had already been produced which aimed to support teachers' attempts to develop children's use of information and reference books in this authentic way (Wray, 1991). These materials work through the ubiquitous primary school 'project' and provide activities which require children involved in project work (for which it is assumed they have some motivation and enthusiasm) to identify, locate, consult, extract information from and evaluate reference materials. The materials thus give teachers a means of directly teaching particular aspects of information handling through authentic and motivating children's activities. They also provide guidance on strategies by which teachers can make contextualised assessments of children's abilities in these information skills. These materials were a model for other materials which have been produced, trialled and developed during the project.

THE PROJECT IN ACTION

During the project we evolved a way of working with teacher groups which appeared to be mutually beneficial. This consisted of the EXEL team leading an initial day's course for between fifteen and twenty-five teachers who expressed an interest in the project's aims. Following this initial day, the teachers involved contracted to trial in their classrooms some of the activities and materials we worked through with them. They were given some support in this, either from our own resources (which locally involved us working alongside them in their classrooms on a fairly regular basis), or from the resources of the local authority. This typically involves the local adviser or advisory teacher working with them. In most authorities some mid-term group meetings also took place to encourage the sharing of experiences. Follow-up days enabled a more general sharing of ideas and examples. The project then was almost entirely school and classroom-based. From the remainder of this book the reader will get a clear sense of this as we provide a multitude of classroom examples and it is hoped that this feature makes the book a very practical document for teachers of reading and writing.

The classroom-based nature of the project is also important in another way, however. Through working closely alongside thoughtful, and often inspiring, teachers, we have come to realise just how important this form of collaboration is. With these teachers we have been engaged in a very elaborate joint construction of working theory to explain and develop the tentative ideas with which we began the project. Each idea presented in this book has been extensively tested in a range of classroom settings and each has been significantly developed by the teachers who have used it. This investment of teacher energy and practical wisdom in the project has been largely responsible for the immense impact it has had. As such, we feel that the project represents something of a model for curriculum development.

THE PROJECT'S MAIN FINDINGS

Obviously the rest of this book will outline the project conclusions in much more detail. At this point, therefore, we shall do no more than briefly describe what we feel have been the two most significant theoretical contributions of the project. These emerged from the project's work but have become very significant underpinnings to its operation.

Without a doubt the most important feature of our work has been its concentration on helping children read non-fiction texts more effectively. This is largely the result of the interests expressed to us by participating teachers. As well as developing a range of strategies through which teachers might develop the non-fiction reading and writing skills of their children, we have developed a model to describe the process of learning from text (explored more fully in Chapter 4). We have christened this the EXIT model (EXtending Interactions with Texts) and its major feature stems from a realisation on our parts that the period a reader is actually in physical contact with an information book ('when the eyes are on the page') is only a part of the process. Of equal importance are what happens before the reader uses the book ('before the eyes meet the page') and what happens afterwards ('after the eyes leave the page'). The stages in the model are given below, with alongside each an example of the kind of question which readers might ask of themselves when engaged on this stage. It should be stressed that we do not intend this model to be interpreted as a linear description of what happens when we read for information. Rather, the process is recursive with various stages being revisited and tackled in different orders dependent upon the precise purposes of each reading experience.

The EXIT model

1 Elicitation of previous knowledge. (What do I already know about this subject?)
2 Establishing purposes. (What do I need to find out?)
3 Locating information. (Where and how will I get this information?)
4 Adopting an appropriate strategy. (How should I use this source of information?)
5 Interacting with text. (What can I do to help me understand this better?)
6 Monitoring understanding. (What can I do if there are parts I do not understand?)
7 Making a record. (What should I make a note of from this information?)

8   Evaluating information. (Should I believe this information?)
9   Assisting memory. (How can I help myself remember the important parts?)
10 Communicating information. (How should I let other people know about this?)

A second part of our work has been to develop a model to underpin an approach to teaching the extended, purposeful literacy we have been exploring. The model of teaching we found most useful owes a great deal to that put forward by Australian theorists such as Frances Christie and Joan Rothery (see Derewianka, 1990) and is based upon a curriculum cycle of:

• teacher modelling/demonstration,
• joint activity,
• independent activity.

We have argued for the inclusion of a further stage of assisted activity in this cycle and many of the teaching strategies we have been exploring operate at this stage of the process, being aimed at the 'zones of proximal development' of the children being taught. This teaching model and the rationale for it are explained in Chapter 3.

Chapter 2

The state of literacy

Schools, and how and what they teach, are subject to frequent scrutiny at both the informal and the formal level. In the constant efforts to foreground good practice, improve standards, initiate change, adopt new ideas, conform to government directives and provide the best education they can for our pupils, teachers are often on the receiving end of reports which offer them advice and point them towards areas of concerns with the curriculum. This is an inevitable part of the process of being involved in teaching in an open and publicly funded system and, as literacy is central to education, there is no shortage of research, statistics, surveys and reports on the current position of literacy in the primary school.

In this chapter we will look at reading and writing in primary schools as portrayed in a variety of official and academic reports, expanding the brief review of these which we gave in Chapter 1, and, alongside this, we will consider evidence from classroom teachers, currently working in schools. From this complex mass of information we hope to highlight the areas of progress in literacy teaching and learning and areas which still give cause for concern.

The area of particular concern to us is the evidence relating to the use of non-fiction texts in the classroom. Until recently there has been a tendency to regard this as an area of literacy teaching that was the concern of the junior teacher and although we will challenge this view we will begin by looking at the evidence as it relates to Key Stage 2.

CONCERNS ABOUT READING AT KEY STAGE 2

Concerns about the teaching of literacy beyond the early stages are not new. As we noted in Chapter 1, almost twenty years ago HMI found 'little evidence that more advanced reading skills were being taught' (DES, 1978, para. 5.30). Their 1989 report on reading policy and practice comments that,

> Schools saw it as an important obligation to help pupils master the complexities of advanced reading, but while they saw it as their duty, few

gave coherent accounts of what these skills were and how they were to be developed.

(DES, 1989, para. 36)

It is interesting that this report acknowledged that teachers, as well as HMI, recognised the problem but were unsure how to solve it. We will return to this shared recognition of the problems when we come to examine teachers' views later in the chapter.

The same concerns about developing reading continue to be found in the most recent annual inspection review of English. One third of schools achieving 'good standards' implies the presence of two thirds of schools who do not achieve the systematic development HMI consider praiseworthy.

> Pupils achieve good standards of reading in about one third of schools where they build on and develop systematically the skills they have learnt at Key Stage 1 in skimming, for example, or in deduction or in using the texts for information. The variety of their reading increases, they talk about it in structured ways and use reading regularly for an increasing range of purposes such as information seeking.

(OFSTED, 1995, p. 8)

Interestingly this latest report implies that reading for information does begin at Key Stage 1 and our work certainly shows that infant children, with support and scaffolding, can become effective readers and writers of non-fiction texts.

Often official reports such as those quoted above make clear that children's reading of fiction texts is relatively well developed, as in these comments from the 1990 survey: 'Reading for pleasure is widely encouraged. . . . During their primary years most children have good literature presented to them by their teachers' (DES, 1990, p. 9). The perceived problems therefore seem to focus on what are often called 'advanced reading skills' and in particular the reading of a wide range of non-fiction material.

CONCERNS ABOUT WRITING

We can trace a similar trail of well recognised and reported problems relating to the teaching of writing. The 1978 HMI report's comments quoted in chapter 1 identify the lack of a range of writing (para. 5.36) and the extensive use of copying (para. 5.33). More recent reports reveal that such problems continue to occur. 'Standards of writing . . . in about 50 per cent of schools standards overall in KS2 were relatively poorer than in KS1. They were depressed by excessive copying, and lack of demand for sustained, independent and extended writing' (OFSTED, 1993, para 9).

In their 1990 survey HMI noted that,

> In the course of their day to day work children devoted much time to writing. . . . Narrative and descriptive writing in prose were almost

universal, writing associated with topic work often entailed excessive copying from reference books, the incidence being highest with the 11 year old children. Although the older, abler children were capable of using writing to argue a case, to express opinions, or to draw conclusions, most of them had little experience of those kinds of writing.

(DES, 1990, p. 5)

Note again in this comment the implication that, as with reading non-fiction, writing in a wide range of genres is the preserve of the 'older, abler children'. We will challenge this view throughout this book.

CONCERNS ABOUT TEACHERS

As with the issues arising from official reports into reading and writing in the primary years certain issues relating to teachers themselves also trace a continuous thread throughout successive reports. We quoted earlier from the 1991 HMI report in which the view was expressed that many Key Stage 2 teachers were unaware of 'how far removed their current practices were from the requirements of the National Curriculum'. Teachers lack of subject knowledge and expertise is another recurrent theme:

in the immediate future schools need to help teachers to acquire more knowledge and expertise in relation to:
- knowledge about language – its structures, functions and variations
- teaching writing.

(OFSTED, 1993, p. 23)

Or again in the 1995 annual summary: 'There are some persistent weaknesses in teachers' knowledge and expertise: (including) ... the development of reading at Key Stage 2' (OFSTED, 1995, p. 7).

Official reports seem to lead to the conclusion that for the majority of schools the curriculum demands in English, beyond the initial stages, seem to have set some targets which many schools are finding very difficult to meet, in part because of teachers' need for increased knowledge and in-service provision. But what do teachers themselves see as the current state of literacy? We will now go on to look at teachers' own accounts about what goes on in their classrooms and what strengths and problems they perceive in the teaching of literacy.

TEACHERS' VIEWS

It is important that amidst the welter of official reports the voice of the classroom practitioner should be heard. What do teachers themselves perceive as their aims, strengths and problems in the teaching of literacy in the primary school? One key aspect of the EXEL project was to develop curriculum practices and materials which would be of help in developing children's interactions with texts and it was therefore important that we should first discover, from teachers themselves, those areas in which they felt they lacked expertise. We therefore began the project by undertaking a survey of primary teachers to elicit their current practice and views relating to literacy. Several interesting trends emerged from this data which gave us some indication of how teachers view literacy and their role in promoting it, the areas of the language curriculum they are able to talk about with confidence, those areas which they see as problematic and, revealingly, those areas of literacy development which were barely mentioned by teachers.

The survey

One hundred and seven teachers were surveyed using a questionnaire and a sub-sample of twenty of these teachers were interviewed at length using a semi-structured interview schedule. The teachers were drawn from a cross-section of schools ranging from large, inner-city schools in London and Devon to small, village schools in Devon. The teachers involved had a range of teaching experience from two years to over twenty years. Most were teaching children at Key Stage 2 although there were three Year 7 teachers as our sample contained two middle schools. The interviewed teachers were a random subset of the teachers who responded to the questionnaire. Some of these teachers were language postholders whilst others were teachers who agreed to be interviewed but who had no special brief for language within their school. Seventy-five per cent of the sample were female and 25 per cent were male but no marked gender differences became apparent in the analysis of responses.

Literacy activities

The teachers who took part in the survey showed a very high level of consensus over practices that they regarded as useful in promoting literacy and over three quarters claimed to use the following highly rated activities on a regular basis of more than once a week:

- project work,
- sustained silent reading,
- prediction activities,
- story writing,
- reading stories to children,
- using word processors,
- reading non-fiction to children,
- collaborative writing.

This high degree of regard and usage must of course be treated with some caution. It is possible that our inclusion of an activity in the questionnaire implied that it had some value and we must also be aware of the possible mismatch between what people say they do and what they actually do. However, with these provisos in mind, the information is revealing in what it shows about change and continuity in classroom practice over the last decade and in what is not included.

Change and continuity in practice

Several clear trends emerged from both the questionnaires and interview data which evidenced changing practice. Certain practices now appear to have become widespread within our schools. In reading the most striking was the use of some form of regular, sustained silent reading sessions (claimed by 91 per cent of the sample). This can be contrasted with the much lower incidence of this activity found by Southgate *et al.* (1981) and suggests a major change in classroom practice over the past twenty years. The use of the word processor as a tool for writing and the use of collaborative writing is now well established.

Other activities still seem to be almost universally employed by teachers which suggests a fair degree of continuity in practice. Predominant among these were reading aloud stories to children and asking children to write stories for themselves. Both of these were claimed as regular classroom practices by all the teachers in the survey, the only two activities so universally mentioned. They are testament to the overwhelmingly strong position of fiction in the experience of modern primary children. As we were embarking on a project targeted at the reading and writing of non-fiction texts, this was, of course, a finding of some significance to us.

There were some activities that revealed far less consensus as to their perceived usefulness. Just over half of the teachers, for example, found comprehension exercises useful (55 per cent) but a very significant minority (35 per cent) found them not useful. Several of these felt moved to write or underline the word 'exercises' in expressing their views about these activities. This perhaps suggests that they considered comprehension important but exercises not the most useful way of tackling it. One source of our own interest with the area of extending literacy was a disquiet regarding the effectiveness of perhaps the most commonly used activity for the specific development of reading for understanding.

The teaching of reading

Junior teachers clearly see reading as an important responsibility and it is clear from the detailed interviews that all teachers see their role in the teaching of reading as more than just enabling the children to be able to decode the text. When asked about their aims in the teaching of reading all the interviewees mentioned a range of aims but some teachers revealed a narrower view of reading than others.

Seven main kinds of aims were mentioned by the twenty interviewees. These were, in order of the number of teachers mentioning them:

- increasing children's independence and/or confidence in reading (20),
- getting children to enjoy reading/love reading/become interested in books (19),
- developing the range of children's reading (10),
- developing reading for information/study skills (7),
- development of creativity/imagination (5),
- teaching specific reading skills, e.g. phonics (4),
- development of critical thinking (2).

Virtually all teachers (19/20) mentioned enjoyment. They saw developing a pleasure in books as the key to a child's continued reading – as one teacher put it 'I want children who are able to read and do read – who want to read.' As part of developing this love of reading teachers mentioned extending children's knowledge of a wide range of authors and genres, the importance of discussing and sharing books with children, the importance of allowing children to develop their own tastes and choose their own books.

Less than half mentioned encouraging children to see books as sources of information and some mentioned study skills and/or higher order reading skills. This reaffirms the foregrounding of fiction in classrooms about which we have commented earlier.

Most of the teachers in the survey felt that they had to use a variety of strategies to develop reading. Eighty-two per cent of them disagreed with the statement that 'once children have mastered the basics of reading all they need to develop their reading is practice', which suggests they were very well aware of the need for deliberate teaching of reading beyond the decoding fluency stage.

Many strategies for teaching reading were mentioned which implies that teachers have a large and varied repertoire and is perhaps evidence for the beneficial effects of initial and in-service teacher education. Strategies which were widely mentioned included:

- paired/shared reading
- reading to, sharing books with parents/other adults
- reading instructions/worksheets
- research skills
- visits from authors/illustrators
- reading aloud to an audience
- children reading their own work to the class
- reading environmental print
- looking at other languages

- taped stories to listen to
- interactive displays
- book reviews
- peer tutoring
- discussing books
- reading records with children's comments
- cross phase reading partners
- group reading.

From these we can see that reading is no longer regarded as a solitary activity undertaken by children in isolation, or with a teacher. Rather, children are encouraged to read in a variety of contexts and with a variety of people. Reading is not viewed as a static solitary activity but is now viewed as a much more active sharing process. It would not be true to say, however, that private reading is not still also encouraged. The desirable image of the individual child 'lost in a book' still has a powerful appeal for teachers. All of which does suggest that children in present day classrooms are probably getting a much richer experience of reading than their forebears of a generation ago.

There were some problems mentioned by the teachers in terms of their teaching of reading and most of these are very predictable. When the twenty interviewed teachers were asked about their problems fourteen of them immediately mentioned resources or books. This, of course, reflects a very real and justifiable concern and one which is unlikely to have been significantly alleviated over the three years since this survey was carried out. To put it into perspective, however, it has to be said that at work here there is probably a very large, and long overdue, raising in expectations on the part of teachers. Few visitors to classrooms over the past twenty years can fail to have been struck by the increased attention schools have given to the quality of their resources for reading. Publishers have responded by increasing the standard and range of the materials they produce. As examples of this, as beginning teachers in the 1970s we were faced in our classrooms with a book supply which consisted of a few, rather dog-eared hardback copies of, mainly, Enid Blyton books and rather more copies of the various levels of Wide Range Readers. The equivalent nowadays, in the worst equipped schools, will undoubtedly be better in terms of range and quality.

Other problems mentioned by the interviewed teachers included those of coping with children with a wide range of special needs (12 teachers), the shortage of time in the school day/week (11), a lack of specific teaching expertise either within the school or in themselves (6), the pressure from parents (6), and problems within children such as lack of motivation, poor vocabulary and so on (4).

The teaching of writing

One section of the survey focused specifically on writing and teachers were asked about their aims in developing children's writing, any significant problems that concerned them in this area and the teaching activities and materials they currently used.

Although over 95 per cent of the teachers questioned agreed strongly with the comment that 'Children need to write for a range of audiences and in a range of styles in order to become effective writers', it was significant that, in the subsequent interviews when they were asked to talk about their aims and their problems in the teaching of writing, most teachers tended to concentrate their replies upon the writing of narrative texts. The writing of specifically non-fiction texts was, in fact, mentioned by only 15 per cent of the sample. About 55 per cent did talk about the need to introduce children to a range of texts. Having articulated this awareness, however, the teachers went on to list only a limited range of text types and again these were almost invariably 'fiction' – poetry, different types of stories, etc. There were a few teachers (20 per cent) who mentioned non-fiction writing but only in broad terms relating to other curriculum areas such as writing in science or in history. Only one teacher mentioned any non-fiction text type by name (identifying 'reports' and 'explanations'). This suggests a lack of knowledge of the range of texts and, at the least, the lack of a shared vocabulary with which to discuss text types. It supports the hypothesis of OFSTED that teachers need to improve their own knowledge about language in this area.

One problem mentioned by teachers in the survey, in relation to writing, (excluding the universal problems of time and resources mentioned by almost 100 per cent of the sample!) was that of helping children move away from copying. As one teacher put it, 'I always try to encourage them to write in their own words but you still find children taking it straight from the page of a book.' This echoes the OFSTED concern about 'excessive copying'.

This measure of agreement between what teachers themselves and school inspectors see as the problems to be tackled in the writing of non-fiction texts has also been borne out by our work with teachers over the last three years.

CONCLUSION

The findings of our survey of teachers echo those arising from a review of the relevant literature. It does seem that fiction texts are given an overwhelmingly predominant position in many primary classrooms, both in terms of what gets read and what gets written. Teachers are much more secure in their understandings about how to develop children's fiction reading and writing than they are about non-fiction. These two factors appear to be mutually reinforcing in a kind of spiral. Teachers are unsure of exactly how to teach non-fiction reading and writing, therefore they tend to focus their attention on what they understand a lot about, fiction. Children are given much more access to fiction texts to read and are encouraged to write largely in fictional forms. Because children's diets are relatively meagre in terms of non-fiction, teachers get a much reduced opportunity to work out for themselves strategies for supporting interactions with non-fiction texts or for making judgements about criteria for and levels of success in these interactions.

What we have been attempting to do through our work in the EXEL project is to break into this spiral by working directly with teachers to develop their understandings about the nature of non-fiction reading and writing and their repertoire of strategies for teaching with it.

Chapter 3

Towards a model of teaching literacy

In this chapter we shall outline the ideas about learning and teaching upon which the work of the EXEL project was based and try to relate these to teaching approaches used. We shall begin by examining what we feel we have learnt from recent research into the nature of learning. We shall then go on to discuss a model of the teaching process and try to illustrate this by describing some teaching activities. These activities will be dealt with in greater detail later in the book.

WHAT DO WE KNOW ABOUT LEARNING?

Four basic insights into the nature of the learning process have come from research over the past decade or so. Each of these has important implications for approaches to teaching.

Learning is a process of interaction between what is known and what is to be learnt

It has become quite clear that, in order to do any real learning, we have to draw upon knowledge we already have about a subject. The more we know about the subject, the more likely it is that we shall learn any given piece of knowledge. Brown (1979) has described this as 'headfitting', by which is simply meant that the closer the distance between what is already known by the learner and the particular information to be learnt, the more likely it is that learning will be successful. Learning which does not make connections with our prior knowledge is learning at the level of rote only, and is soon forgotten once deliberate attempts to remember it have stopped. (Most people can remember times they learnt material in this way, usually as preparation for some kind of test: once the test was over, the information 'went out of their heads'.)

Learning has been defined as 'the expansion and modification of existing ways of conceiving the world in the light of alternative ways' (Wray and Medwell, 1991, p. 9). Such a constructivist approach to learning places great emphasis upon the ways in which prior knowledge is structured in the learner's mind and in which it is activated during learning. Theories about this, generally known as schema theories as they hypothesise that knowledge is stored in our minds in patterned ways (schema) (Rumelhart, 1980), suggest that learning depends, first, upon the requisite prior knowledge being in the mind of the learner and, second, upon it being brought to the forefront of the learner's mind.

Learning is a social process

Ideas about learning have progressed significantly away from Piaget's purely 'lone scientist' view of learners as acting upon their environments, observing the results and then, through reflection, modifying or fine-tuning their schema concerning these environments. Modern learning theory gives much greater recognition to the importance of social interaction and support and posits a view of the learner as a social constructor of knowledge. In collaboration with others, learners establish:

- *shared consciousness* a group working together can construct knowledge to a higher level than can the individuals in that group each working separately. The knowledge rests upon the group interaction.
- *borrowed consciousness* individuals working alongside more knowledgeable others can 'borrow' their understanding of tasks and ideas to enable them to work successfully. Vygotsky (1962) has termed the gap between what a learner can do in collaboration with others and what he/she can do alone, the 'zone of proximal development' and suggests that all learning in fact occurs twice in the learner: once on the social plane and once on the individual.

Learning is a situated process

We learn everything in a context. That is not controversial. But modern learning theorists also suggest that what we learn *is* the context as much as any skills and processes which we use within that context (Lave and Wenger, 1991). Psychologists have sought in vain for 'generalisable skills' and all teachers are familiar with the problem of transfer of learning. Why is it that a child who spells ten words correctly in a spelling test, is likely to spell several of these wrongly when writing a story a short while afterwards? The answer is simply that the learning of the spelling is so inextricably bound up with the context of learning that it cannot easily be applied outside of this context.

There are many instances of this which will be familiar to most teachers. In one class, for example, we encountered a boy who was an expert at quoting horse racing odds but could not manage school 'sums' although the mathematical content of these was actually much simpler. Similarly, many tradespeople like decorators, carpenters, plumbers have to perform very complex mathematical calculations as part of their everyday jobs yet for some mathematics would have been an area of some difficulty when at school. Medwell (1993) reports how, in her research into children's writing, she found one girl who showed no evidence at all of drafting or revising in her school writing and showed no awareness of this when talking about her writing. She was, however, the organiser of a club for her friends at home and had produced a written set of club rules which showed a number of signs of having been revised. She had certainly not transferred her understanding from one context to another.

Learning is a metacognitive process

A good deal of interest has been aroused by the notion that the most effective learners are those who have a degree of awareness about their own levels of understanding of what they are learning. Vygotsky suggested (1962) that there are two stages in the development of knowledge: first, its automatic unconscious acquisition (we learn things or how to do things, but we do not know that we know these things), and second, a gradual increase in active conscious control over that knowledge (we begin to know what we know and that there is more that we do not know). This distinction is essentially the difference between the cognitive and metacognitive aspects of knowledge and thought. The term metacognition is used to refer to the deliberate conscious control of one's own cognitive actions (Brown, 1980). Numerous research studies have examined the operation of metacognition in the reading of children and adults, that is, how successful readers are at monitoring their own comprehension. Overall, there has been a remarkable consistency in the findings of these studies and the two most replicated results have been that:

- 'younger and poorer readers have little awareness that they must attempt to make sense of text; they focus on reading as a decoding process, rather than as a meaning-getting process' (Baker and Brown, 1984, p. 358),
- 'younger children and poorer readers are unlikely to demonstrate that they notice major blocks to text understanding. They seem not to realise when they do not understand' (Garner and Reis, 1981, p. 571).

Arising from such work there has been a strong suggestion that learning can be improved by increasing learners' awareness of their own mental processes.

PRINCIPLES FOR TEACHING

Some clear principles for teaching emerge from these insights.

- We need to ensure that learners have sufficient previous knowledge/ understanding to enable them to learn new things, and to help them make explicit these links between what they already know and what they are learning.
- We need to make provision for group interaction and discussion as teaching strategies, both in small, teacher-less groups and in groups working alongside experts.
- We need to ensure meaningful contexts for learning, particularly in basic literacy skills. This implies some kind of negotiation of the curriculum for learning. What is a meaningful context for teachers cannot be assumed automatically to be a meaningful context for learners.
- We need to promote learners' knowledge and awareness of their own thinking and learning. This might be done by, for example, encouraging them to think aloud as they perform particular cognitive tasks.

TOWARDS A MODEL FOR TEACHING

Palincsar and Brown (1984) describe a teaching procedure which begins from the principles just outlined. Working with the aim of improving students' abilities to respond effectively to text, they begin by arguing that most attempts to train students to do this have produced rather discouraging outcomes, with teaching apparently having little real impact upon learners' use of strategies for making sense of textual materials and, particularly, on the transfer of these strategies to activities outside those directly experienced during the teaching context. They attribute this failure to effect real change in learners' approaches to dealing with text to a model of learning which sees learners as simply responding, relatively passively, to instruction without really being made aware of just what they are learning and why. They claim that teaching, to be successful, needs to encourage learners to be active in their use of strategies and to understand why, and when, they should use the strategies to which they are introduced.

The model of teaching they propose as an alternative is based upon the twin ideas of 'expert scaffolding' and what they refer to as 'proleptic' teaching: that is, teaching in anticipation of competence. This model arises from the ideas of Vygotsky (1978), who put forward the notion that children first experience a particular cognitive activity in collaboration with expert practitioners. The child is firstly a spectator as the majority of the cognitive work is done by the expert (parent or teacher), then a novice as he/she starts to take over some of the work under the close supervision of the expert. As the child grows in experience and capability of performing the task, the expert passes over greater and greater responsibility but still acts as a guide, assisting the child at problematic points. Eventually, the child assumes full responsibility for the task with the expert still present in the role of a supportive audience. Using this approach to teaching, children learn about the task at their own pace, joining in only at a level at which they are capable – or perhaps a little beyond this level so that the task continually provides sufficient challenge to be interesting. The approach is often referred to as an apprenticeship approach and most primary teachers will be familiar with its operation in the teaching of reading (Waterland, 1985). In the apprenticeship approach to reading, the teacher and child begin by sharing a book together with, at first, most of the actual reading being done by the teacher. As the child develops confidence through repeated sharings of the book, he/she gradually takes over the reading until the teacher can withdraw entirely.

The distance between the level at which children can manage independently and which they can manage with the aid of an expert is termed by Vygotsky 'the zone of proximal development' and it is, according to the model of teaching which has begun to emerge from these ideas, the area in which the most profitable instruction can proceed. Vygotsky claimed that 'what children can do with the assistance of others might be in some sense even more indicative of their mental development than what they can do alone' (1978, p. 85).

Most of us will have had experience of being taught in this way, even if those teaching us could not explain their pedagogical theory in these terms. I learnt to drive a car by sitting alongside an expert driver who had over-riding control of the driving mechanisms (the pedals) and was operating these, without my knowledge, to make sure I did nothing likely to dent my confidence. I taught my daughter to swim by walking alongside her in the water and holding her around the middle while she kicked and splashed her arms. Eventually I began to let go for seconds at a time, then minutes until finally she set off across the pool entirely unaided.

There appear to be four stages to the teaching process implied by the model:

Demonstration

During this stage, the expert models the skilful behaviour being taught. There is some evidence that learning can be assisted if this modelling is accompanied by a commentary by the expert, thinking aloud about the activities being undertaken. One relatively simple procedure is that of the teacher modelling how he/she tackles the skills he/she is teaching, that is, reading or writing in such a way that the learners have access to the thought processes which accompany these activities. Tonjes (1988) discusses metacognitive modelling as a way of teachers demonstrating to children the reading and comprehension monitoring strategies which they use and argues that teachers using this approach should concentrate upon modelling mental processes –

what they think as they read or write, rather than simply procedures – what they do. Only in this way, she suggests, can children learn strategies which they can apply across a range of situations rather than which are limited to the context in which they were encountered.

Joint activity

The expert and the learner share the activity. This may begin by the expert retaining responsibility for the difficult parts while the learner takes on the easy parts, while in some teaching strategies prior agreement is reached that participants will take turns at carrying out sections of the activity. The expert is always on hand to take full control if necessary. One of the best examples of this joint activity is that known as 'paired reading' (Morgan, 1986) in which the teacher (or parent) and the learner read aloud in unison until the learner signals that he/she is ready to go it alone. The teacher withdraws from the reading but is ready to rejoin if the learner shows signs of difficulty such as prolonged pausing or reading errors.

Supported activity

The learner undertakes the activity alone, but under the watchful eye of the expert who is always ready to step in if necessary. In our own work on the reading and writing of non-fiction we have found that this is the stage in the process which is most often neglected and teachers tend to move too rapidly from heavily supporting the children's work to asking them to work without support. Consequently, this is the stage at which most of our practical teaching strategies are aimed.

Individual activity

The learner assumes sole responsibility for the activity. Some learners will, of course, move much more rapidly to this stage than others and the teacher needs to be sensitive to this. It is, arguably, equally as damaging to hold back learners by insisting they go through the same programme of support and practice as everyone else as it is to rush learners through such a programme when they need a more extensive programme of support.

THE MODEL IN ACTION

Reciprocal teaching

A set of teaching procedures based upon this apprenticeship model was designed by Palincsar and Brown (1984) to try to develop the reading and comprehension monitoring of a group of 11 year olds with reading problems.

Their approach used what they termed 'reciprocal teaching' to focus upon four activities:

summarising   asking the children to summarise sections of text, thereby encouraging them to focus upon the main ideas in a passage and to check their own understanding of these,

questioning   getting the children to ask questions about what they read, again encouraging them to attend to the principal ideas and to think about their own comprehension of these,

clarifying   asking the children to clarify potentially problematic sections of text, requiring them to evaluate the current state of their understanding,

predicting   getting them to go beyond the words of the text to make inferences which they must justify by reference to what they read.

Each of these activities had a cognitive and a metacognitive dimension in that not only were the children working upon their comprehension of the texts (comprehension fostering) but they were also having to reflect upon the extent of their comprehension (comprehension monitoring).

The reciprocal teaching procedure involved an interactive 'game' between the teacher and the learners in which each took it in turns to lead a dialogue about a particular section of text. The 'teacher' for each section first asked a question, then summarised, then clarified and predicted as appropriate. The real teacher modelled each of these activities and the role played by the children was gradually expanded as time went on from mostly teacher to mostly pupil.

This procedure was tested on a group of eleven year olds with reading difficulties. These children did initially experience some difficulties in taking over the role of teacher and needed a lot of help in verbalising during summarising, questioning, clarifying and predicting. They did eventually, however, become much more accomplished leaders of the comprehension dialogues and showed a very significant improvement on tests of reading comprehension, an improvement which seemed to generalise to other classroom activities and did not fade away after the completion of the research project. Palincsar and Brown attribute the success of their teaching programme to the reciprocal teaching procedure, suggesting that it involved extensive modelling of comprehension fostering and monitoring strategies which are usually difficult to detect in expert readers, that it forced children to take part in dialogues about their understanding even if at a non-expert level and that they learnt from this engagement.

Gilroy and Moore (1988) report on the results of their replication of the Palincsar and Brown reciprocal teaching procedure with 9 to 13 year olds in New Zealand. They found that positive gains in comprehension test scores were made by these children. In a review of research on the reciprocal teaching approach Moore (1988) agrees with the Palincsar and Brown analysis of the strengths of the approach and suggests that it has a great deal to offer, particularly to children with identifiable weaknesses in reading comprehension.

Meta-reading

As an example of this, here is an extract from one of the classrooms in which we have been working. The class were doing some work on the topic of engines and the teacher was sharing with them a book about this topic. She began by sharing a photocopied extract from the book with a group of children. She accompanied her reading of this text by a commentary explaining her thinking as she worked with its ideas. Here is the first part of her reading (the words in italics are directly read from the text):

> Now, this passage is called *The Steam Engine*. I hope it might tell me something about how steam engines work and perhaps about how they were invented. I know that James Watt made the first steam engine. I suppose the passage might tell me when this happened. I'll read the first sentence or so. *The power developed by steam has fascinated people for hundreds of years. During the first century AD, Greek scientists realised that steam contained energy that could possibly be used by people.* Oh, it looks like the power of steam has been known about for longer than I thought. The first century AD – that's around 1800 years ago. I'm not sure what it means about steam containing energy though. I'd better read carefully to try to find that out.

During this meta-reading, the teacher was concentrating on doing four kinds of things. She was:

- *predicting* looking forward to the information the text might give her,
- *clarifying* working out ideas in ways she could better understand them,
- *questioning* allowing the text to spark off further questions in her mind,
- *summarising* putting the information in the text into a few words.

These four activities were discussed explicitly with the group and written on large cards which were displayed in the classroom. Later, with a different passage, the teacher agreed with the group that they would take it in turns to predict what the passage might be going to be about, to clarify what it told them, to ask questions about what they read and to summarise what they learnt.

Later still, the group were given the task of reading a passage amongst themselves using the same strategies to guide their discussion.

The ultimate aim, of course, was that they would become sufficiently familiar with this procedure for interacting with a text that they were able to adopt it when reading themselves. What they learnt as a social activity would become internalised and individual.

EXTENDING THE SCAFFOLDING

As mentioned above, we have drawn the conclusion from our work in schools that teachers have a tendency to withdraw too quickly the support (scaffolding) they offer to learners who are struggling to master new skills. One of the main emphases of our work has been to find ways in which learners might be given support without the necessity for the teacher to be constantly with them, which, of course, is impossible. We will describe here just two of the support structures we have been using, both of which relate particularly to readers finding and using information from non-fiction texts. Both are described more fully, and illustrated by classroom examples, in later chapters of this book.

KWL grids

The KWL grid was developed as a teaching strategy in the USA (Ogle, 1989) and is a simple but effective strategy which both takes readers through the steps of the research process and also records their learning. It gives a logical structure for tackling research tasks in many areas of the curriculum and it is this combination of a simple but logical support scaffolding that seems to be useful to readers. A KWL grid consists of three columns (see Figure 3.1), the first two of which set the scene for the reading by requiring thought about prior knowledge and just what the reader predicts he or she might learn from the material to be read. The third column acts as a note-taking space.

From extensive use of this strategy we have found two major benefits from it. First, because it begins with the reader's knowledge, it makes the copying out of large sections from the text very unlikely. Second, it seems that children readily recognise the usefulness of the strategy. We have examples of children who, having been introduced to the KWL strategy, continue to use it

What do I Know?	What do I Want to find out?	What did I Learn?

Figure 3.1 The KWL grid

independently because they see its usefulness. Most of these examples are, in fact, children with reading problems for whom the very significant improvement in 'research' work which the KWL inspires is an important motivator.

Writing frames

We have developed the idea of writing frames which simply give the basic structure for a piece of writing by setting out a sequence of cohesive ties to which the writer supplies the content. Again we have found this strategy especially useful for children with reading problems, many of whom have managed through it to produce the most logically ordered and well written pieces of information writing of their lives. Figure 3.2 gives an example of one writing frame which gets children to reflect upon their own learning as they write. Frames are discussed in much greater detail in Chapter 9. (See also Lewis and Wray, 1995.)

Although I already knew that ....

I have learnt some new facts. I learnt that ....

I also learnt that ....

Another fact I learnt ....

However the most interesting thing I learnt was ....

Figure 3.2 A writing frame

CONCLUSION

Although the insights about learning and the model of teaching which is based upon them have been developed in the context of our work on literacy in the primary school, we feel that these ideas have wide applicability. In particular we feel that the four stage description of the teaching process, as well as its incarnation as *reciprocal teaching*, has great potential. There is some evidence that it is the process which parents of young children tend to use quite naturally in their interactions with their children. We would suggest, therefore, that there are great potential benefits in the application of these principles in the teaching of literacy.

Chapter 4

Extending interactions with non-fiction texts

An EXIT into understanding

Central to our work on children's interactions with non-fiction texts has been our attempt to establish a theoretical basis for teaching children how to learn with texts. An essential part of this theoretical base has been a developing model of the processes involved in this learning. In this chapter we shall describe this model, christened the EXtending Interactions with Texts (or EXIT) model and briefly outline the thinking and research underlying its various parts. The model has been extensively revised over the period we have been working on it and has evolved from a critical examination of other models, extensive classroom work with children and many discussions with teachers and other colleagues.

A BRIEF HISTORY OF MODELS

The processes we are discussing here have tended to be described in the literature as 'information skills' and, in that they refer to the processes of locating and dealing with the information given in texts in a range of media, this is a useful description. We are concerned, however, that the use of this term, and linked terms such as 'information reading' and 'study reading', tends to indicate a separation of these ways of interacting with texts from ways more generally referred to as 'reading'. As Cairney (1990) has argued, theories about the understanding of written text which characterise it as a process of information transfer, that is as 'getting the information from the text', are strongly contradicted by more recent conceptualisations of the reading process as one of transaction, that is, the active construction of meaning in negotiation with the text as written (see Goodman, 1985; Rumelhart, 1985). Thus any model aiming to describe the process of interacting with expository texts must account for its transactional nature and build in a strong element of the reader contributing to the constructed meaning. As Margaret Meek puts it, 'Until now we have sometimes assumed that information books might do children's thinking for them. Instead even the simplest text to be read for information "retrieval" (whatever that is) implies a complex network of interactions and intertexuality' (Meek, 1995, p. 21).

The above remarks notwithstanding, almost all the attempts which have so far been made to elaborate more fully what happens when we read and learn from expository texts have tended to term themselves as descriptions of the 'information process'. This is not to say that all these attempts have nothing to offer a more extended and interaction-based description of this process. Many of the elements described in information skills models have relevance to interactive models of the reading to learn process.

There have certainly been no shortage of models (or, more usually, lists of skills) put forward with the intention of helping teachers plan more thoroughly for their teaching of children's use of textual information. Of these models, two have been particularly influential in our thinking around this issue. The first was an attempt to describe the 'information process' in terms of six stages of activity (Winkworth, 1977). These six stages were used by Wray (1985, 1988a) to form a basis for advice to teachers on the teaching of information skills through class project work. The stages were:

1   Defining the subject and the purpose of the enquiry,
2   Locating information,
3   Selecting information,
4   Organising information,
5   Evaluating information,
6   Communicating the results.

This formulation was used, in a slightly amended form, by Tann (1988) who, in discussing teaching through project work, defined information skills as:

a)   Identifying the information that is wanted,
b)   Selecting possible sources of information,
c)   Locating the information,
d)   Extracting and recording information,
e)   Interpreting/integrating/interrogating information,
f)   Presenting findings.

Both of these six stage models are useful as a guide for teachers of the processes through which their children might go as they pursue project enquiries. They both suffer, however, from the major problem that they are certainly incomplete. They lack what we now feel to be the crucial element of the actual interaction with a text. In the terms of these models, what happens when a reader faces the words on the page of an appropriate text is limited to selecting, extracting and recording information. As argued earlier, this now seems inadequate as a description of the multi-faceted transaction between a reader, coming to a text with a whole range of attitudes, feelings and arrays of knowledge, and the words on a page, created by an author with a range of intentions many of which go beyond the simple passing on of information. They also lack any attempt to help the reader foreground any information they may already know about a topic.

A second formulation of the information process which has been widely quoted and used, particularly in secondary school contexts, was that of the Schools' Council working group under the chairmanship of Marland (Marland, 1981). Marland's group tried to break down the process of a secondary school pupil carrying out an assignment involving the use of information. They suggested nine steps, which were phrased as nine questions, as follows:

1   What do I need to do?
2   Where could I go?
3   How do I get to the information?
4   Which resources should I use?
5   How shall I use the resources?
6   What should I make a record of?
7   Have I got the information I need?
8   How should I present it?
9   What have I achieved?

A particular strength of the way these steps are formulated is that, as pupils are asked questions as they proceed with their assignments, they are given the opportunity to consider directly the processes of their own learning and thinking. They are therefore encouraged to take a metacognitive stance on their own activities, a feature which, as will be argued later, is a necessary part of serious attempts to extend learners' control over their own thinking with texts. The nine questions are still, however, inadequate in their reduction of the text–reader transaction to, 'How shall I use the resources?'

Because of such problems with existing models of the learning with text process, we felt we needed to reconceptualise this process. The EXIT model represents the state of our thinking at this point.

THE EXIT MODEL

In presenting the model we are immediately faced with the difficulty of representing a complex and essentially recursive set of processes in the two-dimensional space defined by print on paper. Although in what follows the model will be represented as a series of numerical stages, it is important to realise that this is for convenience only. We do not intend to imply that this model has to be slavishly followed through in a linear fashion. All interactions with texts in order to learn will involve a much more complex amalgam of mental processes than a simple linear list of stages.

We see the process of learning from, with and through texts as involving ten kinds of mental activities. Each of these 'stages' can, following the Marland model, be expressed as a question and so be available to children themselves as a guide for their thinking. This full model is given in Figure 4.1.

We shall give a brief description of and rationale for each of the ten 'stages' and also, briefly, give some indication of some appropriate teaching strategies. These teaching strategies are discussed in detail in the following chapters.

1 Activation of previous knowledge

It has become quite clear, as we discussed in the previous chapter, that, in order to ensure real learning, we have to ensure that learners are able to draw upon knowledge they already have about a subject. The more learners know about a subject, the more likely it is that they will learn any given piece of knowledge. Learning which does not make connections with our previous knowledge is learning at the level of rote only and is soon forgotten. Any

EXIT: Extending Interactions with Text

Process stages	Questions
1. Activation of previous knowledge.	1. What do I already know about this subject?
2. Establishing purposes.	2. What do I need to find out and what will I do with the information?
3. Locating information.	3. Where and how will I get this information?
4. Adopting an appropriate strategy.	4. How should I use this source of information to get what I need?
5. Interacting with text.	5. What can I do to help me understand this better?
6. Monitoring understanding.	6. What can I do if there are parts I do not understand?
7. Making a record.	7. What should I make a note of from this information?
8. Evaluating information.	8. Which items of information should I believe and which should I keep an open mind about?
9. Assisting memory.	9. How can I help myself remember the important parts?
10. Communicating information.	10. How should I let other people know about this?

Figure 4.1 The EXIT model: stages and questions

model, therefore, which attempts to act as guide for teachers to develop their children's abilities to learn from texts, must include an emphasis upon the need to activate what the learners already know about the topics of these texts. In practical terms this might be achieved through engaging children in discussion, brainstorming and subsequently concept-mapping what they know about a topic, or in the use of KWL grids (What do I Know?, What do I Want to Know?, What have I Learnt?) (Ogle, 1989).

2 Establishing purposes

A crucial part of the process of learning from texts must involve the specification of just what information is required from these texts and why. If this is not done, then subsequent interactions with texts will tend to be haphazard rather then purposeful. For many primary school children, however, an initial purpose for reading will often consist of nothing more than a vague statement such as, 'I want to find out about dinosaurs (or birds, or trains, etc.)', which is certainly not precise enough to be useful to them. Statements like this have two logical consequences. First, they give no criteria for judging the usefulness of any information which is found. If it is about dinosaurs (or birds, etc.) then it must be relevant. Second, there is no indication of when the process of finding information should stop. Children could go on for ever finding information about dinosaurs, etc. and still be no nearer satisfying this vague purpose.

Children need to be encouraged to specify as precisely as possible what it is they want to find out, and what they will do with that information when they have found it. They may be asked to draw up a list of questions to which they want to find answers, or tasks which they aim to complete. A more useful purpose might be something like this: 'I want to find out the relative sizes of the most common dinosaurs so I can draw scale pictures of them on a wall chart'. This defines the area and clearly specifies what they will do with the information once they have found it.

One of the original National Curriculum statements of attainment for English, level 3 (DES, 1990) stated that children should 'Devise a clear set of questions that will enable them to select and use appropriate information sources and reference books from the class and school library.' Such question-setting is itself not unproblematic, but its key function of making work with non-fiction texts more purposeful is of undeniable importance. We should bear in mind, however, that question-setting may not always occur at the beginning of a project. The EXIT model is not intended to be seen as linear in its operation and it is quite likely that question-generation will occur and reoccur as the project progresses.

3 Locating information

Clearly in the world outside school, the texts which will help meet the reading purposes children have defined will not be simply presented to them as a package. They will need to find the information they require in libraries, books, or whatever sources are appropriate. This will involve knowing how to use a library system to track down likely sources of the information required, how to find information efficiently in books and other sources, but also how to use the most important information resource – other people. To this list must also be added the skills of using the various tools of information technology to retrieve needed information. Teletext televisions, information systems such as the internet, and computer data-bases are all extremely useful sources of information in the classroom, but not unless the children possess the requisite skills for using them.

Such location skills are not complicated, yet children and adults alike often seem to have difficulties in using them. From our own research (Wray and Lewis, 1992) it is very common for children to be able to explain perfectly well how to use an index to a book, for example, but then, when left to their own devices, to prefer to leaf through a book instead. There appears to be a problem of transfer of learning here as the children we studied had certainly been taught about locating information in books and libraries. They had just not transferred this knowledge into action. We would suggest that the solution to this problem is to make sure that children are taught to locate information within the context of actually doing it, usually as part of an investigative project and the case studies we describe in Chapters 11 and 12 give clear examples of how teachers might undertake teaching at the 'point of use'.

4 Adopting an appropriate strategy

Efficient readers modify the ways they read according to their purposes for reading, the nature of the texts they are faced with and the context in which they interact with these texts. Compare, for example, the different ways the following reading tasks would usually be approached:

(i)   Finding a telephone number in the Yellow Pages.
(ii)   Reading a newspaper over the breakfast table.
(iii)   Studying a text book chapter in preparation for a test.

In the first example, the reading would involve glancing over several pages of text looking for a particular word or group of words. When this was found, a closer reading of the particular item of information would follow. This reading strategy we generally refer to as 'scanning'.

In the second example, the major part of the reading would involve the rapid browsing through large portions of text, gaining a fairly general picture of what the items and articles were about. Some of these items would probably receive more detailed attention than others, but most would not be read in close detail. This approach to reading is usually termed 'skimming'.

The third example is very different in that it would probably involve the close reading, and perhaps re-reading several times, of every word in the chapter. Such 'intensive reading' is comparatively rare in non-educational settings, but where it is appropriate, it is usually very important that it is done effectively.

From research into the capacity of readers of various kinds to monitor and control their own reading behaviour (Wray, 1994) it appears that one of the things which distinguishes effective from less effective readers is the ability to take appropriate, and conscious, decisions about which reading strategy to adopt in which circumstances, and when to switch strategies. This suggests that if we want young readers to become more effective, we need to give some attention to helping them widen their control of a range of reading strategies. Children need to 'be shown how to read different kinds of materials in different ways' (DES, 1990, p. 31) but also to make decisions for themselves about the appropriate strategies to use in particular situations. We suggest that an important teaching strategy towards this is for the teacher to demonstrate appropriate ways of behaving, that is for the teacher to model how he or she reads a particular information source, thinking aloud as he or she does it so that children can gain an understanding of how and why reading strategies are selected.

5 Interacting with text

The above processes are, we would argue, crucial to the effective use of reading to learn and, in many ways, the success of the actual 'eyeball-to-text' part of the process depends upon them. Nevertheless, it is the stage of interacting with the text which remains at the heart of the whole process. Here the reader engages in an intricate transaction with the printed symbols, constructing a meaning, or meanings, on the basis of what he or she brings to the text – knowledge, beliefs, attitudes – and the intended message of the author of that text. In order to help young readers engage in this process more successfully, we suggest that teachers might employ strategies which focus children's attention on the ways in which texts are constructed and the ways in which their meaning is created and might be recreated. Activities such as cloze procedure, sequencing and text restructuring, given the generic title of DARTs (Directed Activities Related to Texts), have been quite extensively researched (Lunzer and Gardner, 1984; Wray, 1981) and appear to be useful in enabling this interaction with text to happen. Other strategies, such as text marking (by underlining, highlighting or numbering), have not been so widely researched but our, and others' (e.g. Neate, 1992) classroom work suggests they are very useful in helping children focus on the sections of texts most relevant to their reading purposes.

6 Monitoring understanding

Current theories of reading tend to converge in suggesting that an important element of the comprehension process is the reader's ability to monitor their own understanding as it develops in interaction with a text, and to take remedial action in the event of comprehension problems. According to Brown (1980), such an 'aware' approach to one's own reading will involve:

a) clarifying one's purposes for reading, that is understanding the explicit and implicit demands of a particular reading task,
b) identifying the important aspects of a text,
c) focusing attention on these principal aspects rather than on relatively trivial aspects,
d) monitoring on-going activities to determine whether comprehension is taking place,
e) engaging in self-questioning to check whether the aims are being achieved,
f) taking corrective action if and when failures in comprehension are detected.

Reading for meaning therefore involves the metacognitive activity of comprehension monitoring, which entails the use of what have been called 'debugging' skills (Brown, 1980).

Although mature readers typically engage in comprehension monitoring as they read for meaning, it is usually not a conscious experience. Brown (1980) distinguishes between an automatic and debugging state. Skilled readers, she argues, tend to proceed on automatic pilot until a 'triggering event' alerts them to a failure or problem in their comprehension. When alerted in this way they must slow down and devote extra effort in mental processing to the area which is causing the problem. They employ debugging devices and strategies, all of which demand extra time and mental effort. Anderson (1980) suggests that efficient readers need not devote constant attention to evaluating their own understanding and he suggests the existence of an 'automated monitoring mechanism' which 'renders the clicks of comprehension and clunks of comprehension failure'. As fluent readers we will all have experienced such occasions, when we suddenly find ourselves stopping mid read and mentally saying, 'I didn't understand that bit.'

Realising that one has failed to understand is only part of comprehension monitoring; one must also know what to do when such failures occur. This involves the making of a number of strategic decisions. The first of these is simply to decide whether or not remedial action is required. This seems to depend largely upon the reader's purposes for reading (Alessi, Anderson and Goetz, 1979). For example, if a reader's purpose is to locate a specific piece of information, a lack of understanding of the surrounding text will not usually trigger any remedial action. On the other hand, if the purpose is to understand a detailed argument, then practically any uncertainty will spark off extra mental activity.

In the event of a decision to take action, there are a number of options available. The reader may simply store the confusion in memory as an unanswered question (Anderson, 1980) in the hope that the author will subsequently provide sufficient clarification to enable its resolution, or the reader may decide to take action immediately, which may involve rereading, jumping ahead in the text, consulting a dictionary or knowledgeable person, or a number of other strategies (Baker and Brown, 1984).

Numerous research studies have examined children's monitoring of their own comprehension and it is possible to draw some fairly firm conclusions. According to Garner (1987),

> The convergent findings from recent research can be summarised: Young children and poor readers are not nearly as adept as older children/adults and good readers, respectively, in engaging in planful activities either to make cognitive progress or to monitor it. Younger, less proficient learners are not nearly as 'resourceful' in completing a variety of reading and studying tasks important in academic settings.
>
> (p. 59)

It seems that one important area upon which the teaching of reading to learn needs to focus is children's awareness of their own understanding as they read. As with the adoption of an appropriate reading strategy, we suggest that the most effective teaching strategy for this is for teachers actively to demonstrate to children their own thinking/monitoring processes as they try to understand a text. It has been demonstrated that the systematic use of such thinking aloud can have significant effects upon children's abilities to understand what they read (Palincsar and Brown, 1984).

7 Making a record

In adult everyday life, a search for required information will not always result in any written record: the adult may simply remember the information or act upon it immediately. However, in the effective use of reading as a means of study, in schools or colleges, the recording of information, usually by the making of notes, will be an essential part. Yet it appears that even for students in higher education, who have presumably developed effective ways of studying, instruction in strategies for recording information is minimal or non-existent (Wray, 1985). There is a strong argument for the teaching of these strategies, especially note-making, early on in children's school careers (Neate, 1992).

In our attempts to develop effective teaching strategies in this area we have been strongly guided by two principles. One of these concerns the need to consider information recording as inextricably linked to the purpose for reading. It would make little sense to teach children to take notes as they consult information sources without giving consideration to why they will need these notes and to why they are looking for this information in the first place. To neglect the link between purpose and recording is to risk leaving children feeling that they have to note down all the information they read, even if it is only slightly relevant. Sometimes, of course, children will feel they need all the information they encounter and note-making quickly becomes direct copying.

The second principle which has guided us has been that, although skilful adult note-makers might well develop their own note structures to fit particular purposes and texts, younger students will need their initial attempts at note-making quite heavily scaffolded by structures suggested by their teachers. We have been experimenting here with a range of grids and frames to provide this scaffolding (we discuss these in some detail elsewhere in this book) and have found some evidence that children can begin to make their own decisions about note-making as they see for themselves the usefulness of guiding structures.

8 Evaluating information

In the light of the 'information explosion' we are currently witnessing, with the sheer amount of textually stored information growing exponentially far beyond an individual's capacity to be aware of its very existence, it seems even more important that we try to develop in children a questioning attitude to what they read. Many adults retain an inherent propensity to believe that 'if it says it in print, it must be true', yet most would accept that it would not be good for children to be taught to believe everything they read. A useful definition of literacy claims that it involves 'having mastery over the processes by means of which culturally significant information is coded' (de Castell and Luke, 1986: 88). If this is accepted it implies that the literate person, far from being controlled by the manifestations of literacy, should, in fact, be in control of them. This involves having some autonomy in the process of using literacy and having the ability to make choices. Propaganda and publicity rely for their effect upon recipients' lack of autonomy, and their sometimes overpowering influence upon the choices made.

Developing the abilities, and willingness, of children to be critical of what they read will involve encouraging them to use a variety of criteria to judge the accuracy, relevance, and status of the information they find. Children will naturally tend to believe everything they read in books since these books are usually written by adults who know a great deal more than them about a particular topic. Yet they will constantly come across examples of misleading, incorrect, intentionally or unintentionally biased information, and they need to know how to recognise this and what to do about it.

We suggest that one teaching strategy for developing this questioning attitude is for the teacher deliberately to confront children with examples of out of date, biased or contradictory written material and to encourage them to discuss these features explicitly. Obvious possibilities for this include dated books, different newspaper reports on the same events and advertising material. In leading this discussion the teacher can provide a model of how he or she goes about evaluating what is read.

9 Assisting memory

Although more recent psychological research into memory has suggested that this is a good deal more complex than we might at first think, one very influential way of examining memory has been to look closely at its corollary, forgetting. Experiments have revealed that we tend to forget the majority of the facts we try to learn by heart within about twenty-four hours. Our rate of forgetting then slows down considerably and we may maintain our memory of the residue for a much longer period (Ebbinghaus, 1966). Such insights do not provide much cause for confidence that children's location of information in texts will have much long term impact upon their knowledge, a somewhat depressing thought for teachers of heavily content-based curriculum areas such as history and geography. Other research has, however, made it clear that there are factors which can influence memory and forgetting and which can positively inform teaching strategies (Child, 1973).

First, it seems that the more meaningful the information we are trying to remember, the more likely we are to retain it for a longer period. Meaningful information is information which the learner can make sense of, that is, can 'fit' somewhere into a mental map of that part of the cognitive world. This re-emphasises the importance of attempting to bring to the foreground learners' previous knowledge which, as we suggested earlier, is the key to effective learning.

Second, remembering is improved by revisiting the information one is trying to remember. This is well known by teachers who often, in secondary classrooms at least, explicitly ask their pupils to 'revise' material. Often, however, this revision may be too far removed from the initial learning and can turn into an almost complete re-learning. In our work with teachers we have suggested strongly that children need to be given plenty of opportunities to work with information if they are to remember much of it for longer than a few days. This may involve restructuring information into different formats, re-presenting it to other people and using it in different contexts.

10 Communicating information

In many adult information-using experiences, telling other people what has been found is not an important part of the process simply because the outcome may well be some kind of personal action rather than a report of whatever kind. In educational contexts, however, physical outcomes, usually written, are almost invariably expected of children as part of their work with information texts.

There is a very powerful argument that providing children with opportunities to communicate what they have learnt to other people can itself be part of the learning process. Most of us, especially teachers, will have noticed that having to explain things to others often helps us clarify them for ourselves. Language has an epistemic function as well as a communicative: that is, its use creates knowledge in the user. Thus involving children in communicating information to others can be of benefit in helping them make the information they are working with more their own.

Such communication may take the form of writing of one kind or another and we shall discuss strategies for helping children structure non-fiction writing later. There are also, though, a wide range of other ways of communicating what has been learnt, for example, drama, mime, non-fiction bookmaking, oral presentation and two- and three-dimensional modelling. We should also bear in mind that in the complex process of coming to terms with information, creative story making around this information can also be a very important strategy.

CONCLUSION

The purpose of this chapter has been to outline the theoretical basis on which we have been trying to develop teaching strategies to help children respond more effectively to information texts. Although we have been at pains to stress the difficulties in devising models of this nature, we have found that the teachers with whom we have worked have reacted positively to this attempt to provide a framework for their classroom work. We offer it here as a starting point for readers' own deliberations about the nature and teaching of reading for information. In the following chapters we shall look more closely at strategies which allow teachers to intervene and support learners at various stages of the process.

Chapter 5

Activating prior knowledge

In Chapter 4 we looked at the EXIT (EXtending Interactions with Texts) model to examine the processes underlying children's learning from non-fiction material. In the next six chapters we will revisit the model and look at the kinds of teaching strategies that can be used to support and encourage such learning. In this chapter we will look at the prior knowledge children bring to a topic and how we might foreground that knowledge. In Chapter 6 we will look at the issue of question setting and how to develop children's abilities in this. In Chapter 7 we will look at locating and reading information and in Chapter 8 we will look at strategies for helping children to monitor their own understanding as they read and to take notes effectively. In Chapter 9 we will look more closely at the issue of critical reading and suggest strategies for encouraging children in this. In Chapter 10 we will examine strategies for helping children communicate what they have found in effective ways. All of the strategies we will discuss in the following chapters have been extensively used by us, and the teachers working with us, in classrooms that span the age phases. We will show many examples of children's work to demonstrate how the strategies can be adapted for differing age groups.

TEACHING STRATEGIES

In Figure 5.1 we show the EXIT model again but this time with the addition of a third column – teaching strategies. It is these strategies we will now examine.

ACTIVATING PRIOR KNOWLEDGE

The importance of prior knowledge in learning has already been discussed in some detail in Chapter 4. How can we encourage children to recall and use what they already know about a subject?

EXIT: **Ex**tending **I**nteractions with **T**ext

Process stages	*Questions*	*Teaching Strategies*
1. Activation of previous knowledge	1. What do I already know about this subject?	1. Brainstorming, concept mapping, KWL grids
2. Establishing purposes	2. What do I need to find out and what will I do with the information?	2. Question setting, QUADS grids, KWL grids
3. Locating information	3. Where and how will I get this information?	3. Situating the learning
4. Adopting an appropriate strategy	4. How should I use this source of information to get what I need?	4. Metacognitive discussion, modelling
5. Interacting with text	5. What can I do to help me understand this better?	5. DARTs, text marking, text restructuring, genre exchange
6. Monitoring understanding	6. What can I do if there are parts I do not understand?	6. Modelling, strategy charts, grids
7. Making a record	7. What should I make a note of from this information?	7. Modelling, writing frames, grids
8. Evaluating information	8. Should I believe this information?	8. Modelling, discussing biased texts
9. Assisting memory	9. How can I help myself remember the important parts?	9. Revisit, review, restructuring
10. Communicating information	10. How should I let other people know about this?	10. Writing in a range of genres, writing frames, publishing non-fiction books, drama, 2D/3D work, other alternative outcomes

Figure 5.1 The EXIT model: teaching strategies

Discussion

Traditionally, teachers have often begun a topic by initiating a discussion. 'We're going to be looking at the Tudor monarchs. What do you already know about them?' Such discussions are a perfectly acceptable way of bringing children's prior knowledge to the fore. However, discussion is ephemeral – usually no record of what was said remains. Recording prior knowledge, by writing it down, helps us by giving us a note of three important things:

- what our pupils know
- what our pupils do not know – i.e. the gaps in their knowledge
- information about any misconceptions our pupils might hold.

Such information is important for planning purposes, for assessment purposes and for informing a record of what is know/unknown and misunderstood. It also offers the opportunity to make explicit to children, from the very start of an investigation, that they have something to offer and an active part to play, which may help increase their interest and motivation. Strategies to stimulate and record prior knowledge include brainstorming, concept mapping and KWL grids.

Brainstorming/concept mapping

Brainstorming is a simple technique whereby children are asked to contribute orally all they know about a topic. These contributions are noted on a large piece of large paper or the board with either the teacher or a child acting as scribe. Figures 5.2 and 5.3 show fairly typical brainstorms. Brainstorming is best undertaken as a paired, group or class activity, rather than as a solitary activity, as discussion with others can often stimulate further thoughts and links.

Such brainstorms (sometimes called topic webs, word webs, etc.) can then be developed into concept mapping by encouraging the group to look at their initial brainstorm for words/ideas that are linked in some way. For example by using the tiger brainstorm (Figure 5.2) it could be pointed out that 'long

Figure 5.2 The tiger brainstorm

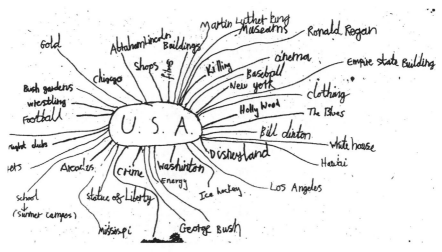

Figure 5.3 A typical brainstorm

jagged teeth' told you something about what tigers looked like, as did the word 'stripes'. The heading 'appearance' could then be introduced and the children invited to add other words into this category (see Figure 5.4).

Not only can the children group words from their original brainstorm but the drawing together of scattered ideas under concept headings often stimulates further ideas (see, for example, Cox and Marshall, 1994) and yet more details can be added to the map. Deriving concept maps from initial brainstorms can also give teachers the chance to introduce more technical vocabulary. For example, the concept grouping 'where they live' which was suggested by the children as they worked on their tiger brainstorm was written down as 'habitat' by the teacher and she explained the meaning of this word as she wrote it. Not only was the group's vocabulary enhanced but they were

Habitat (where they live)	**Tigers**	**Appearance** (what they look like)
India jungle swamp cave zoo		stripes orange/black long jagged teeth big cat claws

Figure 5.4 From brainstorm to concept map

also given access to the more technical vocabulary they were likely to find in the index, headings and text of information books about tigers.

Another way of developing brainstorms into concept maps is for the children to draw in linking lines and write the 'linking idea' along the line that joins two words in the brainstorm. Figure 5.5 shows an example of this from a child's work on fungi.

Alternatively the teacher may start the activity by providing a concept map with headings already in place and invite the children to brainstorm around each heading. Figure 5.6 shows an example of such a blank concept map.

Brainstorming, concept mapping and assessment

Brainstorming and concept mapping can be used before and after a research activity which will allow the maps to be compared. This usually, of course, will show the developments in the knowledge and understanding of a group of children and it does allow for a rough and ready assessment of the group's progress. The concept maps produced after a topic has been completed should, one hopes, show either an increase in the amount children know about that topic, developments in their understanding of the relationships between items of information, or both. Some teachers also find it useful to make a large display item of children's initial concept maps on a topic and to encourage

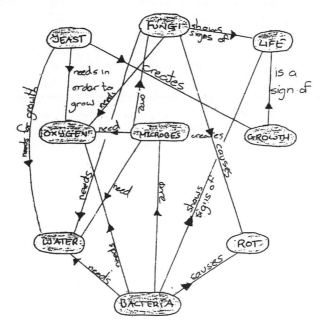

Figure 5.5 A concept map on fungi

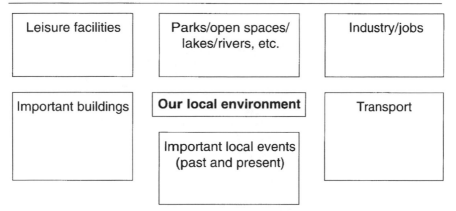

Figure 5.6 A blank concept grid to prompt children's activation of prior knowledge

children to refer back to these to discuss how their understandings have changed during the course of their work.

Alternatively, initial brainstorms can be kept and new knowledge added in a different colour, thus giving children an explicit record of their growing expertise in a particular area of knowledge. Children often take great pleasure in such comparisons as it gives them concrete evidence of how their knowledge has increased in a particular subject (see Figures 5.7 and 5.8).

Asking individual children to concept map a topic at the end of a research quest can also be used to give an insight into children's levels of understanding. An example of this can be seen in Figures 5.9, 5.10 and 5.11. These three children were members of a class which had been studying the topic of coal and as part of their work they had been reading about the ways in which coal is used to make other things. They were asked to show their ideas about the uses of coal in a diagram.

Anthony's diagram (Figure 5.9) suggests that, while he has picked up quite a bit of information from his reading, he has had some problems in making sense of it. If his diagram is to be believed, for example, he is under the impression that TNT is manufactured from nylon!

Susanne, on the other hand, has avoided such problems of categorisation by adopting a simple listing approach to her representation of the information (Figure 5.10). While the resulting diagram is clearly not wrong, it does suggest a fairly literal understanding of what she has read and is equivalent to what Bereiter and Scardamalia (1987) term a 'knowledge retelling strategy' in writing – a strategy they claim is associated with lack of writing expertise.

Gary (Figure 5.11) goes beyond this and seems to adopt what, in writing, Bereiter and Scardamalia would call a 'knowledge transforming strategy'. He has tried to organise the information he has read into categories and, in the

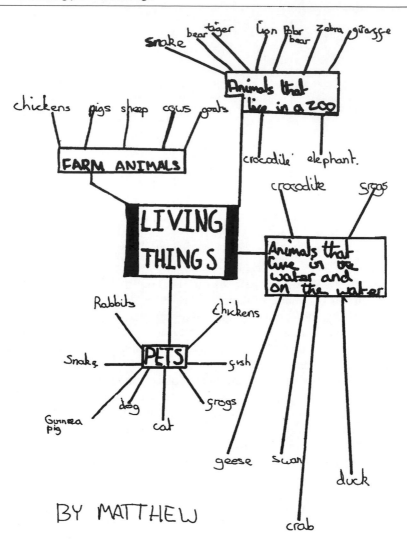

Figure 5.7 Pre-reading concept map on living things

process, has extrapolated ideas from it. The activity of representing information in this way seems itself to have been a learning experience for Gary, very much in the way that Bereiter and Scardamalia see writing functioning for accomplished writers. One imagines, however, that Gary's ingenuity in constructing knowledge to develop what he knew ran a bit thin when it came to the example of paint!

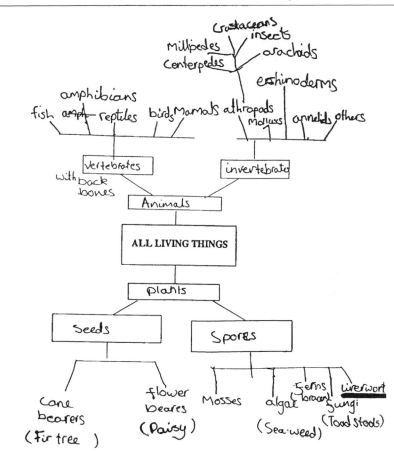

Figure 5.8 Post-reading concept map on living things

KWL grids

Another useful strategy for recording prior knowledge is to introduce children to the use of KWL grids. Each column of such a grid refers to a different stage in the research process. Thus:

K – What do I KNOW about this topic?
W – What do I WANT to know about it?
L – What have I LEARNT about it?

Not only do such grids provide a written record but the format of the grid acts as a structural organiser, helping children see more clearly the stages of their research strategy. The procedure is based on three cognitive steps – accessing prior knowledge, determining what needs to be learnt, recalling what has been learnt. The final column is filled in as a summary point after the children have undertaken some research. It gives children a logical structure for tackling

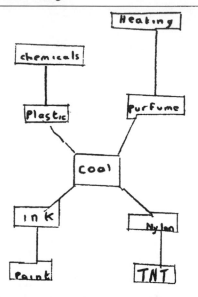

Figure 5.9 Concept map showing faulty understanding

research tasks in many areas of the curriculum and it is this combination of a simple but logical support scaffolding that seems to be so useful to children. The grid provides a simple proforma that helps the children structure their thinking and prompts them into question setting. The grids can of course be

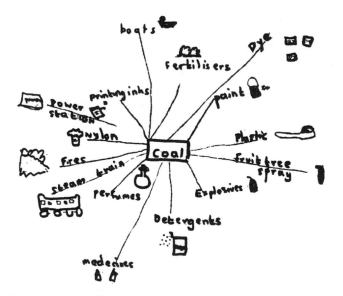

Figure 5.10 Concept map: literal reading

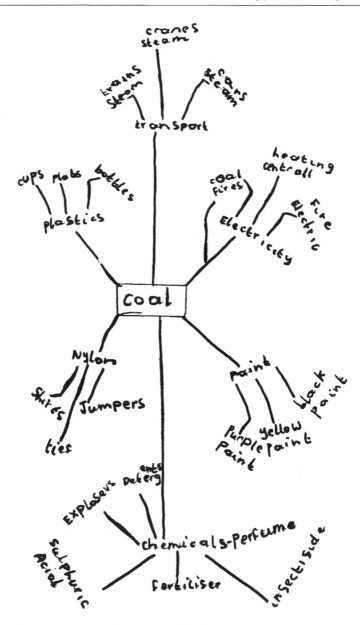

Figure 5.11 Concept map: reading beyond the lines

enlarged and used as group or class grids with the teacher scribing.

Figure 5.12 shows the first two columns of a KWL grid completed by two Year 3 girls working collaboratively to record what they already knew about the Vikings. Notice how this gives the teacher access to some misconceptions

What do I know?	What do I want to know?	What have I learnt?
They had wars. They had maps.	Why did they sail all over England?	
They had dogs. They had longships.	Why did they have horns on their helmet?	
They lived in straw houses. They had fleas.	Why did they have dogs?	
They had helmets.		
They sailed all over England.		
They had shields.		

Figure 5.12 KWL grid about Vikings

('They lived in straw houses,' for example.) Such misconceptions can become the focus for research undertaken by the child for it is important that children play an active role in correcting any misconceptions. Often misconceptions that are merely corrected by the teacher will fail to have much impact upon the children who will simply hold on to them. Children are far more likely to change their minds if they play an active part in correcting their mistakes. A common example of this is a child's spelling error corrected by the teacher but still repeated by the child in subsequent rewritings.

KWFL grids

Some of the teachers we worked with added a further column to their KWL grids – an F column – 'Where will I FIND the information?' Examples and discussion of KWFL grids will be found in Chapter 7.

Using 'concrete manipulatives'

'Concrete manipulatives' is an American term used to cover a range of 'hands on' experiences such as going on trips, using models, handling artefacts, as well as using a range of materials other than books such as videos, computer programmes, or audio tapes. Such materials can be used at any point in the learning process but they can be especially useful in getting children to think about the knowledge they already have about an object and/or subject. The work of Piaget and Bruner, amongst others, has been influential in the widespread acceptance of the importance of such experiences. Recent American research has found that it is a technique still widely used and regarded as highly effective by classroom teachers (Olsen and Gee, 1991). These experiences are most effective when used with discussion. Teachers often use such stimuli as artefacts when they suspect that their pupils might not think that they know anything about a particular topic as in the following example.

What do you know about the Ancient Greeks?

Mindful of the importance of prior knowledge Mr E posed this question to his class.

'Nothing!' was the response.

This kind of response often occurs when children are asked direct questions on some topics which seem remote from their immediate experience. Such replies are misleading for they often indicate not that children really know nothing but that they do not recognise what it is from their own experience that may be relevant to the topic under discussion. They needed help to 'key into' what they know. In such cases teachers often find they need to provide a stimulus to activate children's prior knowledge. When looking at ancient civilisations for example children may know very few details of Greek life but they may know something about modern day Greece and they certainly know plenty about what it is to be a human being – they know that all peoples need food, clothes, shelter, and have beliefs, live in societies, etc. – but they need help in foregrounding this knowledge and then in using that to question how these things may have been different for the Ancient Greeks. Discussion alone would be one strategy to achieve this aim, using concrete manipulatives would be another but on this occasion Mr E used a further strategy.

In pairs or groups children were given pictures with no text. Some, for example, had a picture of a Greek vase, a temple, a landscape, etc. Pictures in books can be used by covering the text with paper or post-its leaving just the picture visible. The children were asked to look closely and list what they could see and what they thought that told them about Ancient Greece. The idea behind this was that in order to make these kinds of deductions they would have to draw upon their previous knowledge. They also made a list of any questions they wanted to ask as a result of their close study of the pictures. The pictures/lists were then passed on to another pair who repeated the process and added further observations/comments/questions. Figure 5.13 shows one child's response to this process.

After some time the text was uncovered, if it existed, and the children checked to see if their observations were confirmed and if their questions were answered in the text. If not their questions became the first piece of research they then undertook.

A similar deductive observation technique can also be used with many artefacts such as old laundry equipment (Victorians, Britain since the 1930's), woven African baskets (study of a developing country) and so on, and can provide an exciting way of activating children's knowledge and stimulating their interest and curiosity.

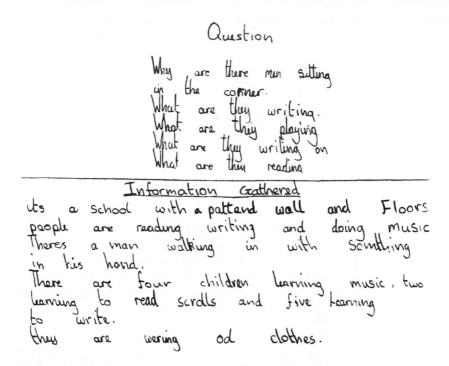

Figure 5.13 Luke's response to the deductive examination of a picture

USING PRIOR KNOWLEDGE STRATEGIES WITH KEY STAGE 1 PUPILS

When working with Key Stage 1 children the teacher will often act as the scribe for the initial brainstorm. Mrs W's class of Year 1 children were about to undertake some work on buildings and were thinking about castles. As they discussed what they knew their comments were scribed by the teacher. They included a knowledge acquired from visits, from television, from information books and from stories. There were several sheets of comments but they included:

Castles are built on hills
They have a moat to keep the baddies out
Castles have towers
A castle is a sort of house
Sometimes they have guards
The guards looked after the leaders
Castles are built of stone
They usually have a princess who is very beautiful
They are built in woods

After listing the comments (26 in all – almost every child contributed) Mrs W helped the children to concept map their comments by putting different coloured dots next to related statements. They grouped the statements according to 'What is a castle?', 'Who lived in castles?', 'What was life like in a castle?' and 'Where were castles built?' Groups of children then decided which aspect they were interested in and copied out 'their' set of comments. See Figure 5.14 for one group's set.

These initial thoughts were displayed in the classroom, along with the linked questions springing from what they knew but wanted to know more about. This initial stage gave the children visual evidence that they already had something to offer, gave the teacher access to their thinking at this stage and allowed their teacher to introduce the written form of the vocabulary they were likely to meet – castle, tower, moat, guard, etc. – when they came to use books. This early introduction to the written form of key words is important for young and struggling readers. As the work progressed the children frequently referred to their original statements and questions. Displaying the process (as well as the final end products of drawings, writing, models, etc.) scaffolded the children's awareness of the process stages by making it explicit and accessible.

FINAL POINT

Although we have focused in this chapter on strategies for getting children to activate their existing knowledge on a topic, it will have become very apparent that almost all the strategies we have discussed also involve children in other parts of the research process. This is inevitable and useful. It reinforces our earlier point that our model of the research process is in no way

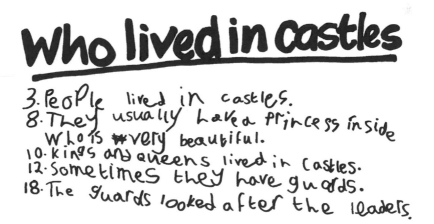

Who lived in castles

3. People lived in castles.
8. They usually have a princess inside who is *very beautiful.
10. Kings and queens lived in castles.
12. Sometimes they have guards.
18. The guards looked after the leaders.

Figure 5.14 An example of the castle comments after having been concept grouped

and teacher assessment. However, encouraging individual or group question setting can be problematic and we shall look at some of the problems related to question setting and at possible ways they might be overcome as well as offering examples of strategies that have proved useful.

Problems in question setting

In our work with teachers over the last three years several common concerns related to encouraging children to ask their own questions have arisen. Whilst most teachers have recognised the motivational aspect of children's own research questions, concerns were often raised in relation to allowing children to set their own questions. These fell into three main categories:

- *Concerns about question generation* 'My students are not used to setting questions. How can I help them?'
- *Concerns about question sense* 'What if they ask silly questions or ones we can't answer?'
- *Concerns about question content* 'Will we cover the National Curriculum content demands if my pupils, rather than I, are setting the questions?'

Concerns about question generation – or 'Any questions?'

Most teachers, if asked, would probably claim that they support the idea of children asking questions in class and encourage their pupils to do so. The research evidence however suggests that children are remarkably unquestioning in class. Tizard and Hughes (1984) drew our attention to the changing role of the child from that of the pre-school child asking many questions of their mother to that of the school child who quickly adapts to the role of being the one who answers questions posed by the teacher. There is much evidence that it is teachers who ask questions in class (French and MacLure, 1981; Tizard *et al.*, 1983; Tyack and Ingram, 1977) and this is reflected in the relatively few studies that have been conducted into children's questioning. Dillon (1988) claims that this is not due to any lack of interest in the subject but that 'investigation can scarcely find any student questions' and in his own study concludes that 'children *qua* students do not ask questions. They may be raising questions in their own minds. ... They may be questioning as they read and study their texts. They may be asking questions of their friends, family and of adults in others roles or contexts. But they do not ask questions aloud in the classroom' (p. 200).

It also seems that many of the questions children do ask in school are procedural questions, provoked by the needs of an activity (e.g. Where's the glue?) rather than 'curiosity' questions (Tizard *et al.*, 1983).

Classroom ethos

It is clear from such evidence that the first thing teachers must be aware of is the need to develop a classroom ethos where question setting is actively encouraged and is met with praise and positive reinforcement. If we think about our own experiences as students it will remind us of the self confidence needed to pose a question in a seminar group – for in doing so we might expose our own ignorance and confusions. An ethos of mutual trust and support, where questions are encouraged and taken seriously, is therefore needed.

Teacher modelling

Teachers can encourage this by providing a model of questioning behaviour and of the type of questions that could be asked. As they read aloud to their pupils, or watch a video together or handle an artefact and so on, teachers can make explicit the questioning that arises in their minds. 'That's interesting. It says the Red Kite is nearly extinct in the wild in Britain. I wonder why? Is it just that species or are others in danger too? It does not tell me here. I'll have to try to find out more about that.'

We should also try to ask open questions of our pupils – What did you think of that? Did it make you want to know more about anything? Open questions are those which encourage children to reflect and query, as distinct from closed questions which merely ask them to reinterrogate the text such as, 'What bird is nearly extinct?' Much has been written about the role of open and closed questioning by teachers and the importance of open questions in developing 'higher order thinking skills' in pupils. We must also remember the importance of teachers 'modelling' such questions and question setting behaviour as a way of inducting children in such activity.

Providing a context

We also need to be aware that questions rarely arise in a vacuum. Just saying 'Right, we're doing a topic on Vikings. Anyone got any questions they want to ask about the Vikings?' may elicit a response but livelier and more searching questions will arise if some initial stimulus is provided. This may be brainstorming around what is already known, listing prior knowledge on a KWL grid, discussing a topic or interacting with a text, such as reading a story or showing a video. All of these activities will help activate the child's existing schema and once the 'filing cabinet drawer' is open and the child's interest engaged many questions will arise spontaneously. In Figure 6.1 we see one small part of the work of an infant, Year 1, class who brainstormed with their teacher all they knew about castles (see Chapter 5). The teacher scribed their responses and then helped them to group their statements together under headings. Their comments were then read back to the class and they were asked 'This is what we already know, what else would we like to know about castles?'

The teacher again scribed the responses. Groups of children were then assigned to sets of questions that particularly interested them and copied these out to make a work campaign plan which was displayed on the wall for all to see. This group question setting is another useful way of supporting children who need some help in generating questions as often it is in active, social situations that someone else's remarks will trigger off a response or query from others in the group.

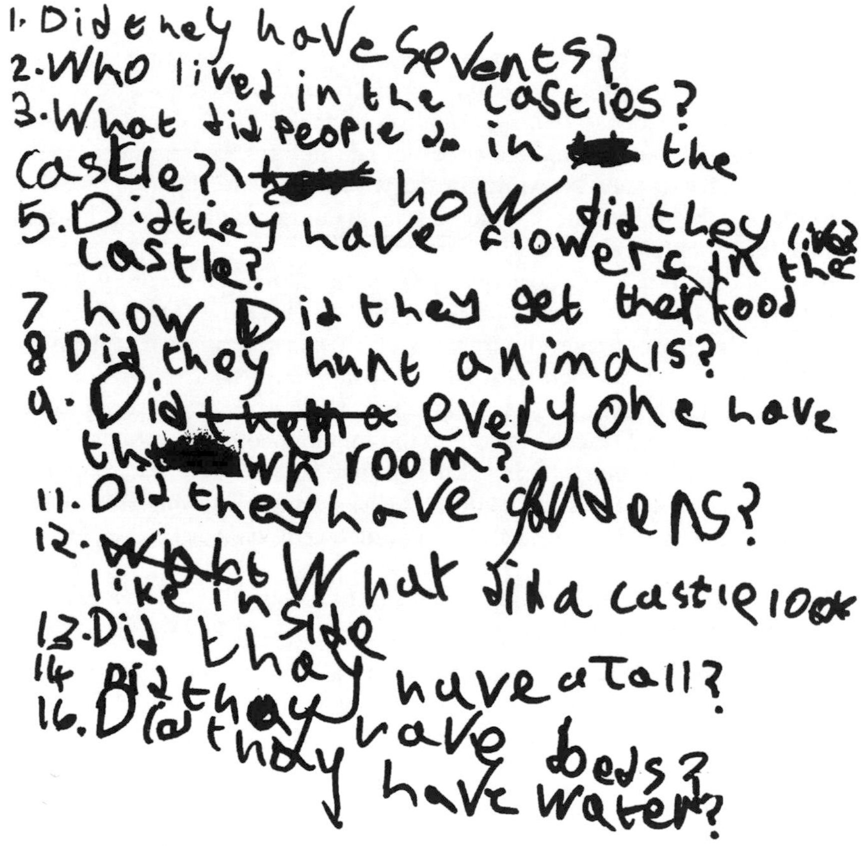

Figure 6.1 Year 1 question setting

Recording questions – using grids

Questions that arise from brainstorming activities can be recorded on a variety of grids and such grids are useful in the organising structures they offer children. Grids help children organise their work by providing a format for recording their questions (and subsequent research) rather than relying on scraps of paper, memory or random pages in their rough work book. The grids are working documents and help the child conceptualise the process stages they are going to undertake.

KWL grids – What do I KNOW? What do I WANT to know? What have I LEARNT? (Lewis, Wray and Rospigliosi, 1995; Ogle 1986; 1989) have already been discussed as a useful strategy for activating prior knowledge. But they also offer a way of recording children's questions. Figure 6.2 gives an example of the questions asked by two 6 year olds about light.

A QUADS grid (Cudd, 1989) consists of four columns – Questions, Answer, Details, Source, and again provides a simple framework for recording information, including the child's questions. A QUADS grid can be introduced immediately after brainstorming. Figure 6.3 shows the QUADS grid of a 7 year old who has raised a wide range of questions in his research into the diplodocus. The class had initially shared all they knew about dinosaurs before each child selected a dinosaur that was to feature in a story they were to write.

An interesting feature of the QUADS grid is the splitting of the answer into

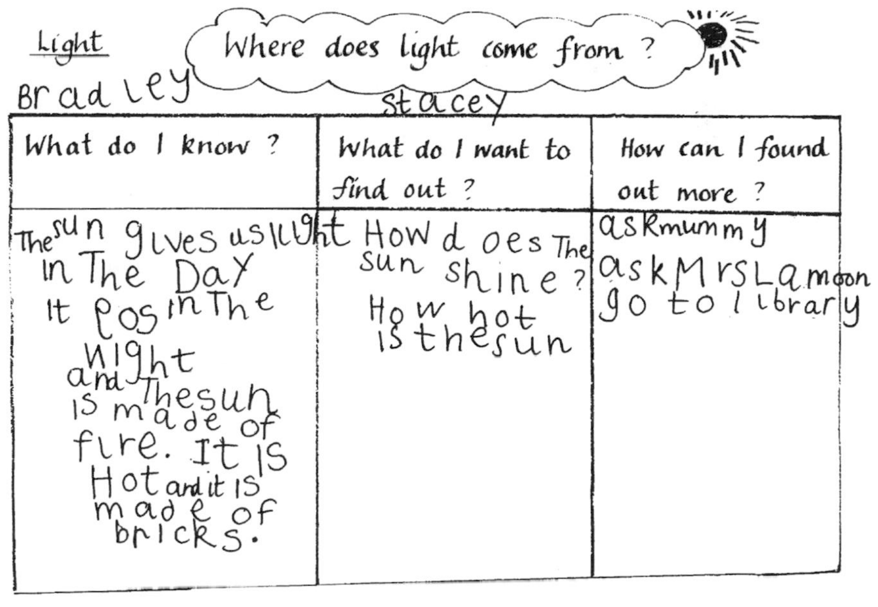

Figure 6.2 KWL grid showing child's questions on light

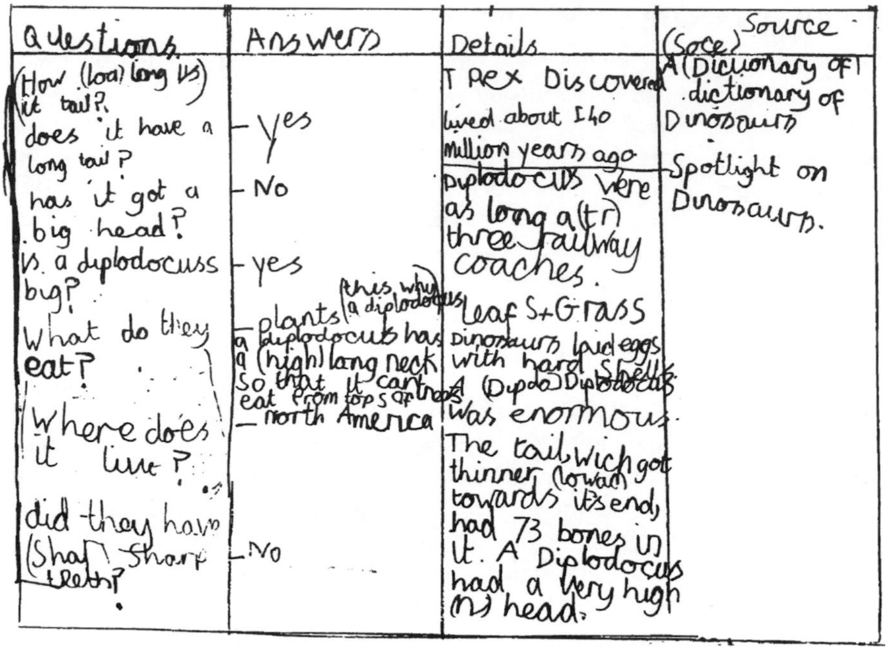

Figure 6.3 Lee's completed QUADS grid on diplodocus

answer/details. This can be discussed with children in terms of the 'short' answer and the 'long' answer. By asking children to think about any information they may have discovered in these terms (short/long) they are asked to summarise first and then give details. This begins to introduce the idea of making a brief note of the key information and is a very useful strategy to guide children away from merely copying down a chunk of information. Look for example at Lee's answer to 'What did they eat?' or 'How big were they?' and see how he has obviously reordered the information he read in the information book he was using.

A further useful study skill habit is encouraged by the inclusion of the Source column. Children are encouraged to note where they found the information in case they need to recheck or need to share it with another. Lee, at 7 and at his first attempt, has not recorded his source fully. He may find it useful to note details such as page numbers, authors of books, for example, but given discussion with and support from his teacher and further opportunities to note down his sources he will undoubtedly refine the skill. He is clearly already beginning to develop his skill at being a researcher.

More structured help in setting questions

Lee had lots of questions he wanted to ask about dinosaurs but there are children who may need more structured help if spontaneous questions do not arise and some children need encouragement to pose particular kinds of questions. There is some research evidence that although children often produce questions that require 'yes–no' answers and also pose many 'what' and 'where' questions, 'why' and 'how' questions are more infrequently asked and 'who' and 'when' questions are least asked (Tyack and Ingram, 1977). The question 'key words' – what, where, why, who, when, how – can be used in a variety of interesting graphic ways to prompt questions and to encourage children to raise the less frequently asked questions. The question words can be listed alongside any brainstorms or 'what I know' statements and the children can be encouraged to match question words to statements. We can see (Figure 6.4) 'what I know' statements becoming questions. So, 'Fishermen hunt whales' becomes, 'Why do fishermen hunt whales?' and this could also have been extended into 'when', 'how' and 'who' questions based on the same statement.

With practise in matching question words and 'know' statements children

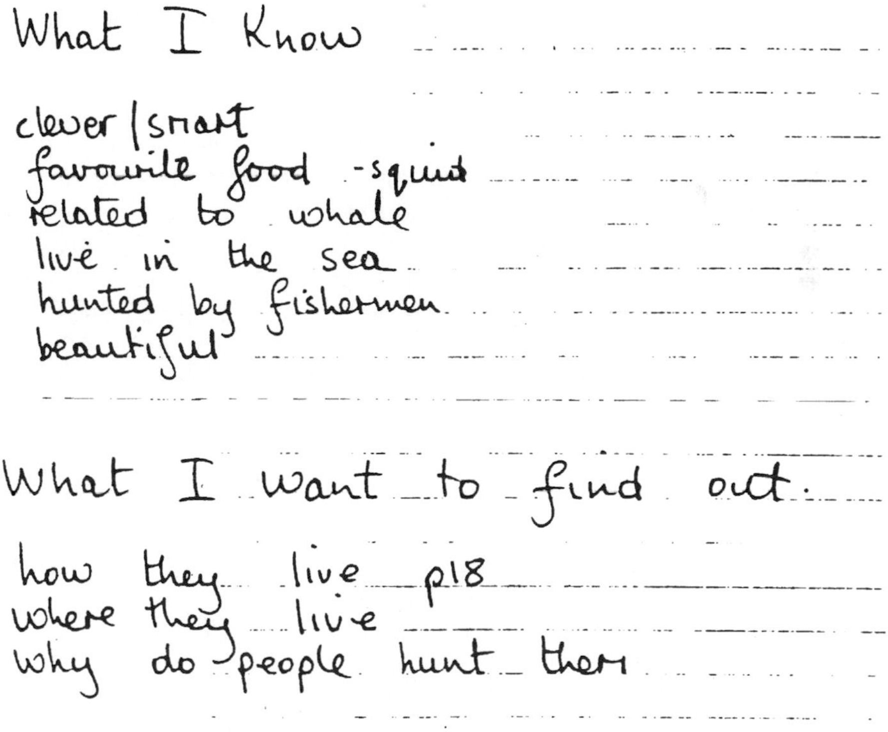

What I Know

clever/smart
favourite food -squid
related to whale
live in the sea
hunted by fishermen
beautiful

What I want to find out.

how they live pl8
where they live
why do people hunt them

Figure 6.4 'Know' statements into questions

move on to being able to turn 'what I know statements' directly into questions without the prompt words to guide them but it may be useful to have a 'question word poster' devised by the children, or jointly with the children, on display in the classroom to act as an occasional reminder when needed.

Various graphic forms can be used to encourage the use of the question words. A 'question tree' can have a branch for each question word. The children then write their question on a leaf and add it to the appropriate branch. Similarly displays can contain a giant 'question hand' with a question word on each finger on which the children can write their questions. Such visual structures – and teachers will be able to think of many more appropriate to varying topics – prompt a range of types of questions and record those questions, producing a useful working document to remind the child of the structure and focus of their research. New questions can of course be added to the display as they arise.

CONCERNS ABOUT QUESTION SENSE – OR 'DOES EATING NETTLES PRICKLE A CATERPILLAR'S TONGUE?'

When Kelly, aged 5 years, asked 'Does eating nettles prickle a caterpillar's tongue?' as she shared a book on butterflies with her teacher and the rest of her class, one can easily imagine the teacher's inward groan – 'How do we answer this one?' – as she scribed the question on to the growing list of questions the class had raised.

This question illustrates one of the dilemmas teachers face when encouraging question setting. Children will often ask questions that are difficult or impossible to answer. We would argue that such questions are not problems but opportunities – opportunities for children to learn important lessons about the nature of questions and the nature of knowledge. They are learning that sometimes we can only give incomplete answers or make reasoned hypotheses, for our knowledge about the world is incomplete or has changed over time or may be controversial. The ability to deal with uncertainties in our world as well as certainties is a crucial lesson. Our tendency to prefer children to ask questions that can be answered easily probably reflects a desire to make the task manageable and successful for the child. Encouraging our pupils to be aware of some degree of uncertainty about knowledge is important in encouraging critical thinking.

There are questions they may fail to resolve but in attempting to find a reasonable answer the child learns that knowledge is not always known or unknown but may lie somewhere on a continuum between the two.

Teachers also expressed concerns to us that children might set 'silly' questions but we perhaps need to ask ourselves – silly to whom? Although children's question might not seem important from an adult perspective they may well be very important to those children, reflecting their interests and life experiences to date. Throughout our work over the three years of the project we did not find a single example of a 'silly' question, in the sense of meaningless. There were, to be sure, several examples of questions which were apparently trivial, but we are conscious that all of us have been in situations where we ask questions which, though vital to us, appear trivial to our companions.

Another type of question which causes concern is that which children set for themselves but to which they apparently already know the answer such as 'Who was Guy Fawkes?' If they were to answer such questions briefly it could appear that they were merely research avoidance strategies. What usually happened in such cases, however, was that the child would immediately fill in the 'short' answer – a man who tried to blow up Parliament – but would then go on to research a more detailed answer (the QUADS grid is useful for encouraging this with its division into answer/details). We can speculate that the opportunity to display some knowledge at the start of a research question has a positive effect in making the task seem accessible.

CONCERNS ABOUT QUESTION CONTENT, OR 'THAT'S A GOOD QUESTION BUT WE'LL LEAVE IT TILL YOU'RE IN YEAR 6'

Perhaps the most often expressed anxiety was whether teachers could afford to let children set questions when there was a prescribed body of knowledge within the National Curriculum which had to be taught to children. This anxiety can be overcome in several ways. First, we need to look at the types of questions children do set themselves and whether they do indeed cover National Curriculum areas of interest. Second, we can adopt approaches to curriculum planning which can help ensure a coverage of all the content knowledge deemed necessary. Finally, we can look at the teacher's role in encouraging specific questions and in including some teacher set questions within a research activity.

Throughout the EXEL project we had many examples of children setting questions that related directly to areas of content in the National Curriculum. When, for example, Lisa and Gary asked 'Why did the Vikings sail all over England?' (see Figure 5.12, p. 50), they were asking a key question from the Invaders and Settlers unit (even if it was rather quaintly expressed!). Children often do ask 'major' questions if we trust them and offer them the opportunity to do so.

Jigsaw planning

Of course not every child will set questions, or undertake research, on every aspect of a particular National Curriculum topic but we can use a jigsaw technique to ensure that within a classroom different groups of children undertake research on different aspects of a topic to share with the whole class at reporting back sessions/expert sessions/hot seating sessions and so on. This kind of organisation ensures that children are given the opportunity to undertake some in-depth research on an aspect of a topic rather than shallow research across a wide range. It also ensures that the same resources are not all required by all the children as different research questions will lead to different information sources.

Teacher's questions and negotiated questions

There may of course be occasions when teachers want to play a more active role in question setting. There may, for example, be a specific misconception or lack of knowledge that teachers have noticed and want the child to address, or the teacher may have planned work on a particular subject and wish to ensure that the children ask the questions that will lead to this subject. It is possible for children to set questions, for teachers to set questions and for teachers and children together to set questions and most research work will contain all these kinds of question setting activities.

Teachers are very good at negotiating questions with children; that is, getting pupils to ask the questions we want them to ask. We are so good at it that we usually are unaware that we are doing it. The following example, from the work of a Year 3 class on farming, shows how this happens. In Figure 6.5 we can see the first two questions a small group of children had discussed and recorded as they began the afternoon's work.

At this point the teacher joined the group. She was happy for them to research their own questions first but she also wanted them to look at what happened on farms throughout the year and to this end she had prepared a calendar grid for children to use later in the session. None of the children had seen this grid. The teacher admired the children's questions, discussed with them how they might find the answers before chatting to them on the topic of farming as she flicked through a book on farming that was on their desk.

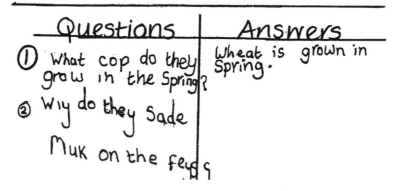

Figure 6.5 The first two questions set independently by the children

She pointed out several pictures of activities at different times of the year and then moved on. When she left the children quickly wrote the remainder of their questions. Figure 6.6 shows the complete set.

The teacher's influence in getting the group to ask the questions she wanted asking is clear. We can see that they had picked up strong messages as to where their teacher's interest lay and had tailored their subsequent questions accordingly. When asked about this interaction at the end of the session the teacher said she had not consciously set out to get the children to ask questions about farming throughout the year but that she obviously must have had her research aim at the back of her mind when she had been talking to children. What she had mentally planned was that she would introduce her questions when the class regathered to share their questions with each other. As it happened she did not need to do this as she had so successfully introduced them earlier. The children seemed to accept the situation with no problems, setting their own questions and being guided into setting others, and we suspect that this interaction illustrates what will always be the norm in classrooms – children set some questions, teachers set others. What we

Questions	Answers
① What cop do they grow in the Spring?	Wheat is grown in Spring.
② Wiy do they Sade Muk on the feds?	
③ What crops do they grow in the Summer.?	
④ what crops do they grow in the Awtum?	they grow potatoes
⑤ what do they grow in the Winter?	

Figure 6.6 The complete set of questions

need to be aware of is that as teachers we have an overwhelmingly powerful influence within a classroom. Children are very good at reading their teachers' minds and will generally try to give us what they believe we want. We must take care, though, that it is not the teachers' questions that always dominate and that end up actually being researched. We must take children's questioning seriously if we are to create an ethos where children regard their own questions as having equal status with those of the teacher.

Questioning misconceptions

On other occasions teachers clearly set the questions from the onset and this is perhaps most important when we have identified a lack of knowledge or a misconception which children's questions do not address. Lisa and Gary had written 'They live in straw houses' in the 'What do I Know' column of their KWL grid about Vikings but had failed to raise any questions about Viking houses in their subsequent question setting (see Figure 5.12, p. 50). On this occasion therefore the teacher set the question 'What were Viking houses like?' and pairs of children researched in a range of information texts about this topic using text marking, listing and labelling to locate and record the information they needed. Finally they wrote reports on Viking houses and we can see how their misconception about 'straw houses' has been corrected (Figure 6.7).

FINAL POINT

In this chapter we have explored a range of strategies for encouraging and helping children to ask questions about a topic. The use of any of these strategies does, of course, depend upon teachers' willingness to involve their pupils in this way. We would argue that the ability to ask appropriate questions is crucial to the role of an active citizen in modern society – therefore children must be given some experience of it during their school years. We do recognise, however, that there is a tension inherent in this. Teachers, quite rightly, are concerned, because of external pressures, about 'getting through the curriculum' ('delivering the curriculum' is the currently fashionable term), and the present curriculum is much fuller than it was. Many will therefore feel that involving their children in setting questions is a time-consuming luxury they can ill afford. In response to this we can do little more than reiterate that the asking of pertinent questions is a vital skill to learn and needs to be addressed somehow in schools. It is, of course, difficult to imagine how children would learn to ask questions for themselves if their teachers always did it for them!

The length [1] of the house
depended on the size of
the family.
There house was not that
coulerful it was mostley
brown. in side it hade
a chest ox drawers and
some other things. ł the
roof had a hole in it
but not all the smoke wo
uld
go out. [2] They had one
big room that they
had to sleep in 'and
eat in. they dident
have coberds for there
food they had barries.
they dident have glass
in there windows.

Figure 6.7 A report on Viking houses

Chapter 7

Information finding and interactive reading

LOCATING THE INFORMATION

Locating the information is often thought of by teachers as being central to the process of using information effectively. We, however, would argue that, although necessary, it is a minor and relatively easy part of the information using process. Locating information includes that part of the process which involves pupils in making decisions about where they might find the required information and then in using specific study skills such as using an index or searching a data base in order to locate the details they need. The problems with this stage of the process lie not with the complexity of the skills involved but in the children's readiness to select and use the appropriate strategy that would enable them to achieve their purpose most effectively. There is evidence (from our own research, described in Chapter 4 and discussed in greater detail in Wray and Lewis, 1992) that children may know how to use an index, consult a library catalogue, use a CD-ROM but that when engaged on a information finding task they often fail to operate such strategies. Instead they may browse through a book, randomly search a shelf of books, ask a friend and so on. Such strategies may be appropriate at times but for the effective location of information they are not helpful. One useful way of explaining this apparent gap between children's knowledge and actions is to distinguish between types of knowledge. One fairly familiar distinction is between declarative (knowing that ...) and procedural (knowing how to ...) knowledge. Paris, Lipson and Wixson (1983) put forward a further category of 'conditional knowledge', that is knowing when, why, where and how to apply particular strategies. Thus we would hypothesise that many children have declarative and procedural knowledge about information retrieval: they know about contents pages, indexes, catalogues, etc., they know how to use these retrieval devices. What they lack is sufficient conditional knowledge to enable them spontaneously to use such devices effectively and efficiently.

We would go further and argue that the mismatch between what pupils 'know' in their heads and what they actually do when confronted by a real task may well be caused by the way in which these skills are taught to children.

TEACHING INFORMATION RETRIEVAL SKILLS

Worksheets

It is very common to find in classrooms, and in publisher's catalogues, books of exercises or worksheets that claim to teach 'study skills'. The quality of such books vary but often they consist of worksheet exercises similar to that given in Figure 7.1. (This sheet is fictitious so as to avoid giving offence to anyone. Readers are invited to check it against worksheets they may have in their schools/classrooms to establish whether the points we make here are substantiated.)

This worksheet is designed to give children practice in using a contents page. They are given an example of a contents page and then asked several questions which require them to use this. After completing several such worksheets children should, it is claimed, now be able to use contents pages and the same process will also hold for other such devices such as index pages. Most teachers will, however, have had lots of experience to contradict

The Contents Page
Here is a contents page:

Contents		
Chapter *Title*		*Page*
1. The Saxon Kings		3
2. William the Conqueror		15
3. The Norman Kings		20
4. The Plantagenets		27
5. The Lancastrians		30
6. The Tudors		34
7. The House of Stuart		44
8. The Hanoverians		50

1. On which page does chapter 4 start?
2. Who is chapter 2 about?
3. Which chapter is about the Norman kings?
4. In which chapter would you find information about Charles Stuart?
5. Which page begins the chapter on the Tudors?
6. Which is the longest chapter?
7. What is the last chapter called?

Figure 7.1 A study skills worksheet

this claim. The reality is that pupils are often skilled at completing such worksheets but fail to transfer the skills to use with real books.

We referred in Chapter 3 to the fairly recent insight that learning is a situated process, that is, it is firmly located in the context in which it initially takes place and the transfer of learning is an extraordinarily difficult thing. In fact, teachers have themselves learnt this apparently universal characteristic of children's learning through their own, sometimes bitter, experience. This suggests that, if we really want to teach children not only about information retrieval devices and how to use them, but also to give them sufficient understanding about the uses of such devices that they are able to make sensible decisions about when and how to employ them, we need to ensure such teaching is embedded in a context as close as possible to that in which the skills will eventually be used.

One way of approaching this is simply to improve the kind of worksheets teachers offer so that at the very least they send children to use real indexes, etc. in real books. Another, complementary way is to embed the teaching of research skills within a real research task and so teach at the point of need.

Worksheets reassessed

It is possible to design worksheets which are more useful than the decontextualised exercises criticised above. Look at the following worksheet (Figure 7.2).

In order to answer these questions the pupil would almost certainly have to consult a 'real' information book. When consulting the book the most efficient way of answering each question would be to look up the key word in the index and then follow up the page references. The worksheet thus gets children using it to engage in 'real' information retrieval. The class teacher would probably plan to use such a worksheet, with a group, within the wider context of a class topic on space and would also be aware that the children using the sheet should be employing the strategy of consulting the index. The teacher could keep an eye on the group as they used the sheet and if it was noticed that they were failing to use appropriate strategies the teacher could join the group to demonstrate how to use an index, etc. This demonstration would consist of showing by example not merely of telling. The teacher would join in and undertake the activity alongside the child/ren, at the same time providing a running commentary on what they were doing. Such teacher modelling, accompanied by an oral explication of the thought processes that underlie the activity is a powerful method of teaching. It makes clear to the pupils what it is an 'expert' does and provides explicit access to the usually invisible thought processes of a skilled text user. It is also a good example of what we refer to as 'teaching at the point of need'.

Space puzzle

Activity 4

The real name of a shooting star is hidden in the pattern below. To discover it, read each of the sentences carefully. If a sentence is true, colour in the spaces you are told to. If the sentence is not true, do not colour in anything.

1 If the name of the largest planet is Jupiter, colour in the spaces marked **4**.

2 If the nearest planet to the Earth is Saturn, colour in the spaces marked **8**.

3 If people who study space are called astrologers, colour in the spaces marked **0**.

4 If the first man in space was called Yuri Gagarin, colour in the spaces marked **1**.

5 If Venus is known as the red planet, colour in the spaces marked **3**.

6 If the nearest planet to the sun is called Uranus, colour in the spaces marked **9**.

7 If the first man on the moon was called Neil Armstrong, colour in the spaces marked **6**.

8 If the moon takes a year to go round the earth, colour in the spaces marked **2**.

9 If Voyager was a manned space ship, colour in the spaces marked **7**.

10 If the Pole star is in the constellation called the Plough, colour in the spaced marked **5**.

1	6	5	4	3	1	6	5	4	0	1	7	3	2	6	0	1	6	6	5	0	6	5	4
4	9	3	8	7	1	7	0	6	2	6	5	7	1	5	9	5	9	8	7	3	2	1	0
6	9	2	8	8	5	8	2	4	3	1	8	4	9	4	8	6	2	0	2	3	7	6	9
5	7	7	9	9	4	9	3	5	7	6	3	2	0	1	7	4	1	6	8	9	8	4	8
1	8	0	3	3	6	0	7	6	8	5	7	8	9	6	3	6	2	0	3	9	8	6	7
6	0	8	7	7	1	7	8	1	9	4	3	2	0	5	2	5	3	7	8	7	0	5	3
4	5	1	6	8	5	4	1	6	0	6	7	8	9	5	0	1	6	5	4	8	9	4	2

Figure 7.2 A contextualised worksheet
Source: The Project Research Pack, © David Wray 1991, Stanley Thornes (Publishers) Ltd

Teaching at the point of need

The demonstration and verbal commentary described above is also a very powerful way of teaching within a real research task. If for example a child has set themselves the question, 'What is rain?' the teacher can work alongside the child/group to scaffold their searching of contents and index for the term 'rain'. In Chapter 10 we will describe in more detail a teacher adopting this powerful teaching strategy as Key Stage 1 children research the details of plants for the school hanging baskets. As well as its strengths as a way of giving children a means of thinking about their actions it is also powerful because it pinpoints teaching to the precise moment at which children are actually engaged in the activity they are learning how to do. They are trying to achieve something (preferably something they value) and the teaching is targeted at helping them achieve this. They do not have to absorb lessons which they then try to apply at some other time.

Using a variety of sources

Children should also be encouraged to think about the wide variety of information sources they may have at their disposal. Books are not the only source of information. Even for adults, asking someone who knows will usually be our first recourse when we need to find something out. We would be doing children a disservice if we taught them that only books were suitable as information resources. They need to be encouraged to use a much wider range: from brochures, pamphlets, posters and magazines to videos, computers, expert people and themselves.

Naturally, encouraging children to use these alternative sources implies that they will have access to at least some of them. In some cases this has financial implications: it is hard to resist the logic which says that for all children to become sufficiently familiar with information sources such as CD-ROMs and computers the supply of these has to be good enough to give each child regular access. In others, it means bringing into the classrooms resources which traditionally have not been found there: fortunately items such as pamphlets, brochures, magazines, leaflets, etc. are generally easily and cheaply available, and can readily be collected by children themselves (see Wray, 1988b for a more extended discussion about resources for information).

One way to encourage children to look at a wider range of information sources is to use a version of the KWL grid mentioned in Chapter 5. A further column can be added making it into a KWFL grid:

K: What do I KNOW?
W: What do I WANT to know?
F: Where will I FIND the information?
L: What have I LEARNT?

This grid encourages the child to plan to use a wide range of information sources ranging from books to people. Figure 7.3 shows the wide range of possible sources recognised by one group of young researchers.

ADOPTING AN APPROPRIATE STRATEGY

Having located information the children then need to read it but, as we indicated in Chapter 4, reading can take many different forms and children need to be introduced to a variety of ways of reading other than the careful reading of every word, from every page, from the beginning to the end of the book that we model so frequently in reading stories aloud to children. As with locating information, teacher modelling accompanied by a running commentary of what the fluent reader, i.e. the teacher, is actually doing, is a powerful way of demonstrating different ways of reading to children. We need to ensure that we read non-fiction aloud to our children just as we read fiction and poetry aloud. One useful set of resources for this are 'big books'.

12/11/93

Kenya

What do I KNOW?   What do I WANT to know?   Where will I FIND the information

What do I KNOW?	What do I WANT to know?	Where will I FIND the information
1 Kenya is a very poor country.	1. How many people live in kenya?	1. In the school Library
2. Lots of crops grow in kenya.	2. What sort of names do you have.	2. Write to the kenya Tourist information centre.
3. They have a church	3. What is your main meal that you eat?	3. Look in an atlas.
4. They carry jugs and bowls of water on their heads.	4. What sort of jobs do you have?	4. Ask Mrs Dingle.
5. It is a very hot country.	5 Why do women do all the hard work?	5. Ask Lisa's uncle.
6 Everybody is black.	6. How many t.v sets do you have.	6. Look in a geography magazine.
7. They have animals to help them grow their crops.	7. What age do people leave school.	7. In Books.
8. Some people live in huts.		8. Leaflets.
9. kenya is in Africa		

Figure 7.3 Recognising a range of sources

Using non-fiction 'big books'

Key Stage 1 teachers are usually very aware of the advantages of using large versions of fiction texts, offering as they do the opportunity for groups of children to be able to see the text clearly, and providing the teacher with a vehicle to model how to use the features of that particular book and how to read it appropriately. Many publishers are now bringing out big versions of non-fiction books aimed at both Key Stage 1 and Key Stage 2 audiences and they provide a useful aid for teachers to model adopting an appropriate strategy by allowing them opportunities to demonstrate a quick skim read, scanning for a specific item of information/name and so on.

Teacher modelling and metacognitive discussion

Using big books or working with a group as they undertake a research task the teacher can demonstrate what it is you actually do – not by merely telling but by showing and accompanying the showing with a monologue of her thought processes. For example one group of children had asked 'How long does a chick stay a chick?' Using the big book version of *The Life of a Duck* ('Magic Beans' series, Heinemann, 1989) the teacher modelled for the group how they might use an information book to answer their question but as she did so she talked about what she was doing and why. She made what is usually an internal monologue accessible to the children. The conversation began something like:

> Now, Joanne asked about chicks growing into ducks. How can I see if this book has anything on chicks? What shall do I do? Shall I read it from the beginning? No, that would take too long? I could look in the index. This list of words at the back that tells me what's in the book. Yes, I can look in the index. Let's look up chicks in the index. So I'm going to turn to the back of the book. Here it is. Index. Now. It's arranged alphabetically a . . . b . . . so c should be next . . . here it is. C. Can anybody see the word chick in this column . . .?

This kind of metacognitive modelling (Tonjes, 1988) – making explicit to the children the thought processes she is going through as she is experiencing them – is giving the children some very important lessons on what it is an experienced reader does. The importance of teachers not simply telling children about the problem-solving, planning and strategic decision-making which characterise the reading process, but actually demonstrating these cannot be over-emphasised. Modelling enables teachers to make explicit the thought processes which accompany involvement in literate activities; processes which, by their very nature, are invisible. Unless these processes are made explicit children can have no way of understanding what it is like to think like an accomplished reader until they actually become one: in other words, much of their learning is directed towards an end of which they have no clear concept.

The teachers explicit vocalisation of the activity provides the children with a 'learning script' which they can 'parrot' when they are trying the task. For, younger and/or inexperienced learners the script often remains explicit – all teachers will have observed young children talking themselves through a task – but as they become more skilled the script becomes internalised and finally operates almost unconsciously only being called to the surface again in tricky situations. A good example of this for adults is in learning to drive. Do you recall your driving instructor talking all the time in early lessons: 'clutch in, change gear' and gradually you began mentally talking yourself through the procedures. Now they are automatic but the script still rises to the surface if you are in certain situations. For example perhaps if you were trying some difficult parking you might find yourself saying to yourself, 'right hand down a bit, reverse, now go forward'.

Simple support strategies

Extra support strategies can be used by less skilled readers or younger children in the early stages of learning to use an index and contents. Children can be encouraged to write the word they are looking for on a piece of card, underlining the first letter. Turning to the index they can then match the first letter with the appropriate alphabetical section before running the card down the section until they match the word. The page numbers can then be copied from the index onto the card. This helps the child recall which pages they need to visit (they can cross out the numbers as they do so) thus helping them hold that stage of the process in their mind without having to constantly turn back to the index. Having turned to the page the children can be helped to scan for the word by running the card quickly over the print looking to match the word they have written. Having located the word the children can then read the sentences immediately before and after the name to see if they contain the desired information.

Other strategies for encouraging scanning and skimming reading are discussed in the section below on text marking.

READING THE TEXT

Actually reading the text is obviously at the heart of the process and a major part of our work in the EXEL project has been aimed at helping children engage in a variety of ways with the information text they have to read. Several of the strategies we have used are those commonly known as DARTs activities (Directed Activities Related to Texts) and they were used and promoted by Lunzer and Gardner (1979; 1984) and their colleagues in a series of Schools Council projects. Because DARTs have been around for some time their usefulness is sometimes overlooked or has been diluted by adaptations that have mitigated against their effectiveness. Cloze procedure, prediction, and sequencing have all suffered slightly from a 'familiarity breeds contempt' effect but they are still highly effective strategies for getting children to pay close attention to meaning.

Cloze

Cloze is an activity in which certain words in a passage of text are deleted and the children are asked to complete the text, as in this example:

Mount St Helens – an exploding mountain

Mount St Helens is a (—A—) in the Rocky Mountain chain of North America. The Rocky (—B—) are fold mountains and form part of the North American plate. To the west of the Rockies lies the Pacific plate and the collision zone between the two (—C—) . The fold mountains were (—D—) as a result of sediments being uplifted from the ocean floor as the (—E—) and North American plates collided approximately (—F—) million years ago.

It is an activity best used in pairs or groups rather than as a solitary activity for its value lies in the discussion of possibilities. Completing a cloze text relies upon the readers actively striving to make the text make sense. They may do this in a variety of ways:

- by using understanding of stylistic features of writing: e.g. at space (A) you could repeat the word *mountain* but would be unlikely to do so as it would mean using it four times in two sentences.
- by using the sense of the whole sentence, i.e. the context: at space (B) reading on to the end of the sentence would prompt the missing word.
- by drawing upon knowledge of language structures (syntactic knowledge): at point (C) the missing word must be a plural noun as signalled by the use of the article 'the' and the adjective 'two'.
- by using existing knowledge: this can be recently acquired, that is, learnt from what you have just read up to that point as at point (E) or, can be information that you simply know or don't know as there is no clue given in the text, as at point (F).

Having finished the passage by working at completing the meaning of a sentence at a time, children should then be encouraged to reread through the whole piece to check the sense of the whole thing. The pairs/groups should then share their choices with the larger class so alternatives can be aired.

This thoughtful struggle to make sense of a text is far removed from exercises such as those in Figure 7.4.

Here missing words have been provided. Indeed in this extreme case the

King Henry 8th had s ___ wives and three children. Having a son was very important to the king as he wanted a son to become k ___ after him. His first child was a girl, M ___ . Her mother was Henry's first w ___ , Catherine of Aragon. Henry decided to d ___ her because she could not have any more children and Henry desperately wanted a son.

Henry divorced Catherine in order to marry Anne Boleyn. Divorce was very rare in those days. When the P___ would not grant Henry the divorce he wanted, Henry left the C ___ church and started the Church of E ___ . In doing this Henry was able to get a divorce from Catherine. Henry's second daughter was Elizabeth. Her m ___ was Anne Boleyn.

Although A ___ had given birth to a daughter Henry still wanted a son and eventually he had Anne Boleyn executed so that he could marry again. This time he married J ___ Seymour who gave birth to Henry's only son. The baby b__ was called Edward. Sadly Jane died soon after giving birth to Edward. After that Henry had three more wives, Anne of Cleeves, Catherine Howard and Catherine Parr but there were no more c ___ .

Words to fit in
Anne boy children Catholic divorce England Jane king Mary mother Pope six wife

Figure 7.4 A cloze exercise

initial letter of each missing word has been retained so all the child has to do is complete a matching exercise. This cloze could be completed successfully without reading the text at all. This 'closed cloze' is far removed from an active attempt to construct meaning and does little or nothing to encourage the child to pay careful attention to the text.

By careful selection of the initial text and thoughtful deletions (rather than deletions according to some arbitrary formula such as every tenth word) the activity can be differentiated for a wide range of abilities and reading expertise.

Sequencing

Like cloze, sequencing can easily be differentiated by careful selection of text and is best undertaken as a collaborative activity which encourages active discussion of meaning. The chosen text is cut up into chunks of several sentences or into individual sentences and the children are asked to reconstruct it into an order which makes sense (which may not be quite the same as the original order – as with cloze, children can often improve upon an author's original text). With younger/less able children it is best to tell them the opening paragraph/sentence but with most children this is not necessary as the game-like conditions of the activity will usually be enough to engage their attention. It is also best to allow children to physically move the text around and try out possibilities.

As part of the EXEL project we videoed several groups of children undertaking cloze and sequencing activities and saw them clearly reading and rereading the text for meaning as they tried out possibilities. In sequencing they used their understanding that the completed piece should make sense to accept or reject various combinations. They clearly understood that the cohesive chains and connectives were crucial and that the overall sense of the passage had to be maintained. Luke and Laura were puzzling over a cut up text about Victorian factories which began with an opening paragraph about the Victorian working day. After trying, and rejecting, one or two pieces to see if they came next Luke saw a connection.

Luke: Ah! . . . Ah! . . . this will go there. Look. (*Points to a sentence in the opening paragraph.*) Look. '16 hours a day.' That would mean working from 6 in the morning to 10 o'clock at night. (*Holds up the next piece he has selected.*) 'Even for **such** long hours . . .' (*Luke's emphasis.*)

Laura: (*Nodding*) Yeah, yeah.

Luke: Yeah. That definitely goes there.

When they had completed the sequencing the whole passage they were questioned about their choices.

Interviewer: How did you know that section went there?

Luke: 'Cos it's still talking about the same thing.

Laura: It's talking about long hours (*pointing to first paragraph*) then carries on talking about long hours (*pointing to next paragraph*).

Throughout the videoed sequence the children puzzled away at the cohesive sense – not always succeeding – but actively working at striving for meaning.

Text marking

Text marking comes in many forms from underlining, writing in the margin, adding symbols to texts and so on.

Underlining

Underlining is a strategy for focusing attention upon particular parts of a reading. It is a strategy that many adults use (albeit badly!) as shown by any book on our book shelves in which we have underlined passages. As owners of books it seems to be a strategy that occurs almost spontaneously when we wish to fix something as being of significance. Of course we cannot encourage children to write on school books but we can use text marking on teacher prepared information sheets or on photocopies of pages from books. However we need to use the strategy in a more focused way than the mass underlining of significant passages.

In Figure 7.5 we see part of some information that children were reading to research Greek gods/goddesses. They were using a variety of colours to underline and therefore differentiate the various family members of Zeus.

Using different colours to differentiate categories of information makes it easier to relocate that information at a later date and also enables multiple marking to take place. Hera, for example, can be underlined as a sister, as a wife and as a resident on Mount Olympus. This kind of text marking – where children search for and underline specific information encourages skimming and scanning. In searching for names, for example, the children would scan the passage looking for words that began with capital letters, whilst in locating the information on the roles of different gods they would quickly surface read until they came to sentences relating to the god they were researching and then they would read this more closely.

Text marking – the main idea/summaries

Pupils can be asked to underline what they think is the sentence that tells you most about X (the main idea of the passage). Different pupils may choose to underline different sentences and this can be used as a discussion point when children share and justify their decisions. In this way they can begin to clarify the author's purpose in writing a text. They can also be asked to underline the most important sentence in each paragraph. Putting these sentences together should give them an outline summary of the whole passage.

Text marking – making notes in margin

Pupils can also be encouraged to write notes in the margins of texts they are studying. They could list out information they have identified, write down any

The Gods of the Greeks
Read the passage below and as you read do the following:

1 Underline the name of Zeus the chief god in red and the name of his main wife in blue.
2 Underline the name of Zeus's brothers and sisters in green.
3 Underline the names of the children of Zeus and Hera in yellow.
4 Underline any other wives and children of Zeus in orange.
5 Use this information to help you complete the family tree and the grid.

Zeus became the King of the Gods after killing his father, Cronus. Zeus lived on Mount Olympus with his chief wife, Hera. She was also his sister. Zeus had two brothers and three sisters. Zeus's brothers were important gods who ruled their own kingdoms. One of them, Hades, ruled the underworld and the other, Poseidon, ruled the sea.

The twelve most important gods lived on Mount Olympus. These included Zeus, Hera, Poseidon and Demeter (a sister of Zeus and the goddess of farming and crops). The children of Zeus and Hera also lived on the mountain. They were Ares, the god of war, Dionysus, the god of wine and Hephaistos, the blacksmith god. Also living there were Apollo, the god of the sun, poetry and music and his twin sister Artemis, goddess of the moon and hunting. Apollo and Artemis were the children of Zeus and Leto.

Three other gods lived on the Mount. One was Hermes, the messenger of the gods and the son of Zeus and Maia, whilst another was Aphrodite the goddess of love. Athene the goddess of wisdom and war was the other. Hestia, the goddess of the home was Zeus's elder sister and she lived on Mount Olympus with her brothers and sisters until Dionysus was given a place there. Hestia gave up her seat to Dionysus.

Figure 7.5 Text marking by underlining

further questions that have arisen in their minds, note where something is not clear to them with a question mark and so on. These activities all help pupils recognise that reading a text is not a passive, one shot activity but involves actively engaging with text in a variety of ways. Figure 7.6 shows the marginal notes made by two Year 3 children as they worked with information about teeth.

Text marking – numbering text to show a sequence of events

Text can also be numbered to identify sequences of events. This is especially useful where steps in a process being described are separated by chunks of

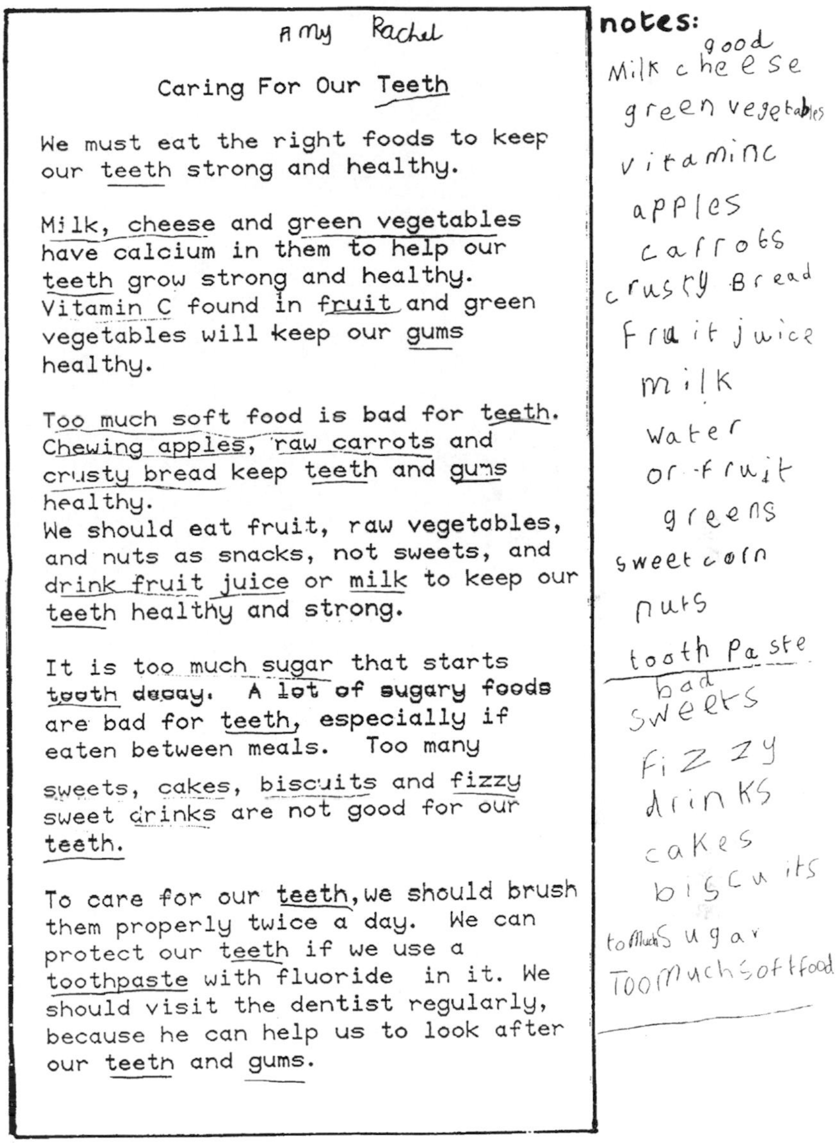

Amy   Rachel

Caring For Our Teeth

We must eat the right foods to keep our teeth strong and healthy.

Milk, cheese and green vegetables have calcium in them to help our teeth grow strong and healthy. Vitamin C found in fruit and green vegetables will keep our gums healthy.

Too much soft food is bad for teeth. Chewing apples, raw carrots and crusty bread keep teeth and gums healthy.
We should eat fruit, raw vegetables, and nuts as snacks, not sweets, and drink fruit juice or milk to keep our teeth healthy and strong.

It is too much sugar that starts tooth decay. A lot of sugary foods are bad for teeth, especially if eaten between meals. Too many sweets, cakes, biscuits and fizzy sweet drinks are not good for our teeth.

To care for our teeth, we should brush them properly twice a day. We can protect our teeth if we use a toothpaste with fluoride in it. We should visit the dentist regularly, because he can help us to look after our teeth and gums.

notes:
good
Milk cheese
green vegetables
vitaminc
apples
carrots
crusty Bread
Fruit juice
milk
water
or fruit
greens
sweet corn
nuts
tooth Paste
bad
sweets
fizzy
drinks
cakes
biscuits
tomuch Sugar
Too much soft food

Figure 7.6 Marginal notes on teeth

texts and children might lose the thread of the basic events. Figure 7.7 shows a text that has been marked sequentially.

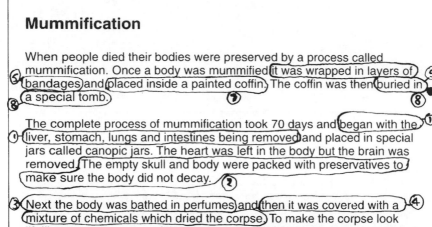

Mummification

When people died their bodies were preserved by a process called mummification. Once a body was mummified it was wrapped in layers of bandages and placed inside a painted coffin. The coffin was then buried in a special tomb.

The complete process of mummification took 70 days and began with the liver, stomach, lungs and intestines being removed and placed in special jars called canopic jars. The heart was left in the body but the brain was removed. The empty skull and body were packed with preservatives to make sure the body did not decay.

Next the body was bathed in perfumes and then it was covered with a mixture of chemicals which dried the corpse. To make the corpse look lifelike some were given false eyes and had their lips and cheeks painted with makeup. Finally the corpse was wrapped and a mask of the person was placed on the mummy. Now the mummy was ready to go in its coffin and be buried.

The Egyptians went to all this trouble to preserve the body because they believed that after death the spirit of the dead person travelled to an afterlife where it would live for ever.

Figure 7.7 Sequential text marking

Group reading aloud

Teachers sometimes use this strategy for fiction texts or playscripts and it is becoming more popular as teachers recognise its potential for scaffolding a close reading of texts. It can also be undertaken with non-fiction texts and can be a helpful way of introducing children to a text that has a high proportion of subject specific vocabulary. If this group reading is undertaken initially as a teacher led activity the teacher can encourage discussion and interrogation of the text as it is shared.

Text restructuring

The essence of this strategy is to encourage children to read information and then show the information in some other way. In doing so they have to 'pass the information through their brain' – that is, work at understanding it. Restructuring thus also gives teachers access to children's levels of under-standing and can be a useful assessment strategy.

There are many different ways of text restructuring (see Figure 7.8). This

Remodelling

- grids
- comparison charts
- fact tree/wheel/others
- listing
- mapping
- maps
- labelling
- diagrams/pictures
- venn diagrams
- genre exchange
    diary entry
    newspaper report
    eye witness account
    fax/telegram
    radio/TV report
    poem
    job description/advertisement
- flow chart
- fact file
- 'trivial pursuit' cards
- board games

Figure 7.8 Text restructuring list

list is by no means exhaustive as teachers and children frequently demonstrate many other exciting ways of restructuring text, but it offers some of the possible starting points.

Sometimes the teacher may provide the format for the restructuring. For example in Figure 7.9 we see the family tree for the Greek gods which the children were asked to complete having undertaken the text marking described in Figure 7.5.

Initially teachers might need to suggest ways of restructuring the text but as the children become used to the technique it can be posed as a very open ended task, i.e. 'show me that information in another way'. For example, having read a text on Roman road building, Gary then showed the information as a labelled cross-section (Figure 7.10). The level of detailed reading of the text he had to engage in order to produce this cross-section is self evident.

Grids, pictograms, graphs, venn diagrams

These are all frequently used as ways of presenting information in another form. In Figure 7.11 we see a grid produced by a child who had amassed a

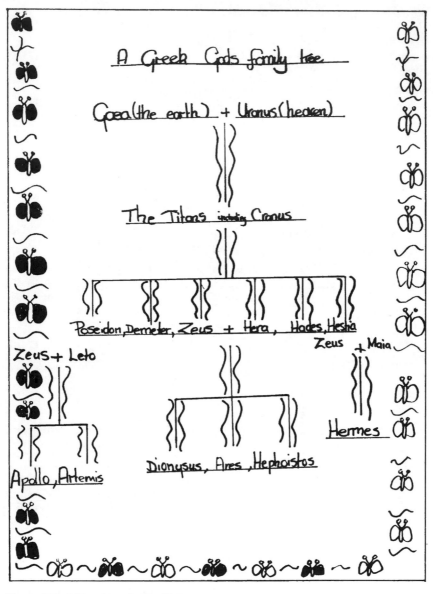

Figure 7.9 A Greek god's family tree

great deal of information on the planets. In deciding the categories for the grid, decisions had to be made about which of the items of information that had been read were relevant and important.

More visual representations can be a useful way of getting younger children to remodel what they have learnt as it enables information to be

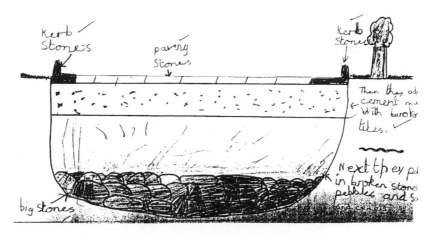

Figure 7.10 Text restructuring – cross-section from a written text

shared without too great a reliance on their ability to read and write. Figures 7.12 and 7.13 show text restructuring undertaken by Year 2 children, in both cases after having shared a book in a group with their teachers.

Planets	How long to orbit	Diameter at the equator	Number of satellites	Mass	Surface temp.
Mercury	88 days	4,878km	0	0.055	350°C
Venus	225 days	12,100km	0	0.815	480°C
Earth	365.25days	12,756	1	1.000	22°C
Mars	687 days	6,780km	2	0.107	-23°C
Jupiter	11.9 years	143,000km	16	318.	-150°C
Saturn	29.5 years	120,000km	21	95	-180°C
Uranus	86 years	52,000km	15	14.54	210°C
Neptune	165 years	49,000km	2	17.2	-220°C

Figure 7.11 Text restructuring – constructing a grid

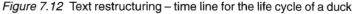

Figure 7.12 Text restructuring – time line for the life cycle of a duck

Matching

Restructuring can also take the form of asking children to apply the information they have read to a different situation. Becky had read about the Beaufort Scale and then drew its sequence and showed the effects of the scale in a particular situation (Figure 7.14). She chose to demonstrate the effects of the increasing wind strengths on a goldfish bowl!

Genre exchange

Restructuring can also take place by asking children to transpose something from one written genre into another written genre. A group of 10-year-olds, for example, had read an expository text about scribes in Ancient Egypt. Normally, perhaps, they would simply have been asked to write about what they had read 'in your own words'. This would most likely have led to a good deal of copying of words and phrases from the original text. This time, however, they were asked to rewrite the information they had gathered into the form of a job advertisement. They examined advertisements in news-

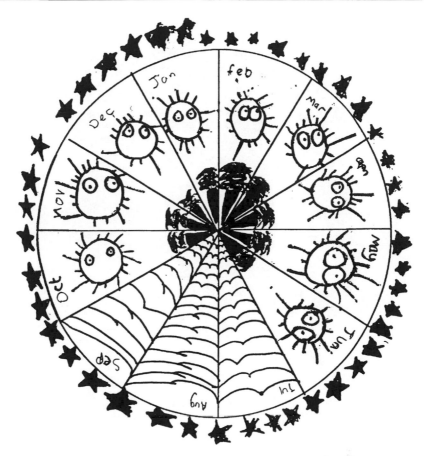

The Nile flooded from July to September.

Figure 7.13 Text restructuring – a pie chart

papers and an example of their writing is shown in Figure 7.15. As can be seen, it is unlikely that this was directly copied; instead the children had had to read and understand the information.

The opportunities for creative use of genre forms are very wide. Some other examples might include:

- summarising an argument in the form of a fax,
- writing a newspaper report about an historical event,
- writing up a science experiment in the form of a recipe,

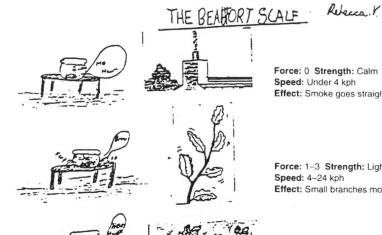

Force: 0 Strength: Calm
Speed: Under 4 kph
Effect: Smoke goes straight up

Force: 1–3 Strength: Light breeze
Speed: 4–24 kph
Effect: Small branches move

Force: 4–5 Strength: Moderate wind
Speed: 25–46 kph
Effect: Small trees sway a little

Force: 6–7 Strength: Strong wind
Speed: 47–74 kph
Effect: Big trees sway a little

Force: 8–9 Strength: Gale
Speed: 75–110 kph
Effect: Slates fall off

Force: 10–11 Strength: Storm
Speed: 111–150 kph
Effect: Widespread damage

Force: 12 Strength: Hurricane
Speed: Above 150 kph
Effect: Disaster

Figure 7.14 Text restructuring – matching experiences

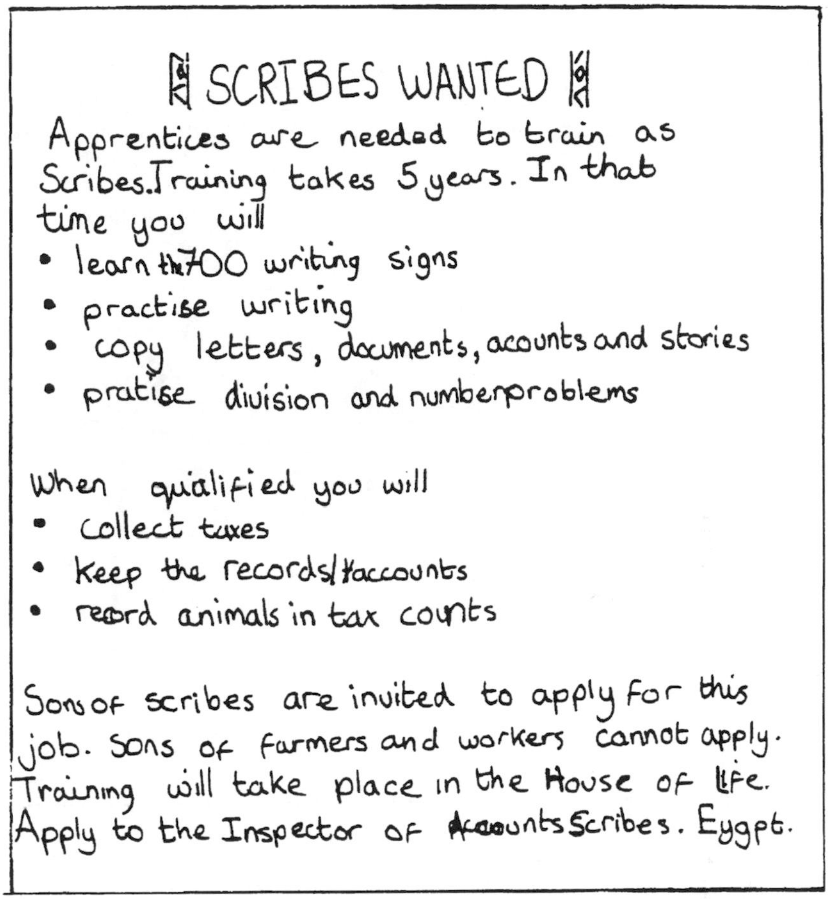

🎋 SCRIBES WANTED 🎋

Apprentices are needed to train as
Scribes. Training takes 5 years. In that
time you will
- learn the 700 writing signs
- practise writing
- copy letters, documents, acounts and stories
- pratise division and numberproblems

When quialified you will
- collect taxes
- keep the records/taccounts
- reord animals in tax counts

Sons of scribes are invited to apply for this
job. Sons of farmers and workers cannot apply.
Training will take place in the House of life.
Apply to the Inspector of Acounts Scribes. Eygpt.

Figure 7.15 Text restructuring – a job advertisement

- writing letters 'home' from a historical event,
- writing an account in the form of a diary.

This 'playing around' with genres not only forces children to reorganise their
material, itself an aid to comprehension, but also gives them vital experience
of the variety of genre forms and guides them away from straight copying of
information they have read.

Restructuring as an assessment strategy

A class of Year 3 children had read and text marked information on the berries
which grow in the hedgerows in autumn. They had been asked to concentrate
on those berries you could eat and those that were poisonous. They had also

been asked to take note of the things which berries could be made into, such as jelly. Their teacher then asked them to show the information they had marked in any way they liked. Some children showed a partial understanding (Figure 7.16), whilst others showed that they had understood that some berries fell into both categories: that is, bad for you when raw, but all right when cooked (Figure 7.17).

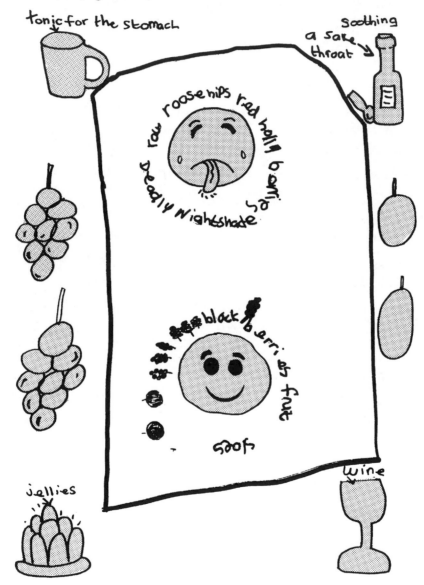

Figure 7.16 Text restructuring as a means of assessment (1)

Figure 7.17 Text restructuring as a means of assessment (2)

By asking the children to show the information in a way they themselves selected, the teacher was able to compare different levels of understanding.

CONCLUSION

The strategies described in this chapter all encourage pupils to engage with the meaning of texts and demonstrate their understanding. Some activities encourage close reading of the text, others, such as text marking, encourage scanning and skimming. It is important that throughout the teacher takes time to discuss with the children what it is they are doing – how they read a particular piece, what decisions they made when undertaking some text restructuring and so on, for this all helps make the process explicit to the pupil.

Chapter 8

Monitoring understanding and taking notes

MONITORING UNDERSTANDING

We discussed in Chapter 4 the importance of children's awareness of their own understanding as they read and suggested that an effective teaching strategy to encourage this awareness is for teachers actively to demonstrate to children their own thinking/monitoring processes as they try to understand a text. Similarly in Chapters 5 and 7 we gave practical examples of teachers engaging in metacognitive discussion as they modelled various stages in the process of research. It has been demonstrated that the systematic use of such 'think alouds' can have significant effects upon children's abilities to understand what they read (Palincsar and Brown, 1984). By 'think alouds' we mean teachers making explicit, by offering a commentary as they read, what it is they do when they understand or fail to understand something.

Having recognised a failure in understanding, fluent readers make decisions as to what they can do to remedy the problem. In school, however, it is common for children in class to ask for help when they do not understand something and teachers often encourage them to do so. If children are to develop as readers, and independent learners, it is important that we encourage them to develop a range of problem solving strategies that they apply first; seeking help only after having tried out solutions for themselves. One way of assisting this process – after modelling such strategies in 'think alouds' is to engage the children in explicit discussion which leads to the joint production of strategy charts. Such charts can then be displayed on the wall and children encouraged to use them when they meet a problem. In Figure 8.1 we see such a chart developed to help children monitor and resolve reading comprehension problems.

What such a chart can do, if the children are encouraged to use it, is to stop a child moving straight from 'I don't understand' to 'Ask someone'. Teachers can use such metacognitive charts (i.e. charts that take children through the cognitive steps to achieve their goal) in many different situations. We have seen such charts developed for spelling, how to locate information, how to use the library and how to overcome certain problems when using the computer,

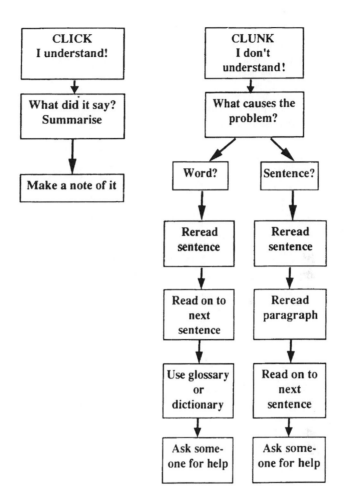

Figure 8.1 A metacognitive chart

to name but a few. We must stress however that such charts are best produced in active collaboration with the children, not merely produced by the teacher and placed on the wall. Once produced, teachers must also constantly draw children's attention to the chart, encouraging their use and parrying all requests for help with 'Have you used the chart?' and only then offering assistance.

NOTE TAKING

The ability to make notes from a variety of sources is an important skill in gathering information and one that is increasingly relied upon as pupils progress through the education system. It is still rare however, judged on our informal questioning of students of all ages to discover many to whom note taking has been actively taught. Most pupils appear to somehow 'pick it up' or 'work it out for themselves'. There are however many ways in which teachers can assist their students become more efficient and effective note takers.

We have already discussed various grids (KWL, QUADS) whose layout encourages note taking but as with all the other stages of the process note taking can be improved by making its operation explicit.

Modelling note taking

Children can be introduced to note taking through teacher modelling. One very effective way of doing this is to start the process by using video material rather than books. This allows the pupils to concentrate on the note taking rather than reading. The teacher sets up a flip chart alongside the television, in full view of the pupils and as they watch the video together the teacher makes notes. Before beginning the focus of the note taking is made explicit: 'We're looking at Tudor food so I'm going to note down anything about food, cooking, meals, etc.'. After the programme has finished the class and teacher discuss it together, with the teacher constantly referring to and using the notes. The notes continue to be displayed to support any subsequent written work. Whilst writing the notes the teacher will be demonstrating the three key elements of note taking:

- summarising, e.g. a section on the food of the poor might be summarised as – little variety, especially in winter.
- deletion, e.g. 'Elaborate dishes were served at banquets' might be scribed in full and then 'were served at' crossed out as redundant in note taking.
- substitution, e.g. long lists can be substituted by single categories, e.g. cabbage, swede, etc., etc. can be noted as vegetables.

Whilst the notes are used in post viewing discussion the teacher can draw attention to the strategies they used. Teacher note taking can be demonstrated several times before the children are then asked to take their own notes from a video programme. It is useful initially to view the video twice, with the notes being made during the second viewing.

Many teachers have found this explicit modelling of great value. It enables them to make the process explicit and it also helps demonstrate the value of note taking for subsequent recall and writing activities. Here, for example, is how Clair Taylor, a primary teacher in Lewisham, has described her use of note modelling to us:

> Afterwards I used my notes and enlarged them as a shared writing activity. As I wrote them I explained what I had written and why, using insertions, arrows, etc. to connect random notes together. This became the basis for a display that gave value to first draft notes and equal status to neat drafts.

After taking notes from video viewing children can than move on to taking notes from text, using text marking as an aid – underlining important points, summarising in the margin, crossing out irrelevant information. For less fluent readers, the text can be read aloud to them for them to either mark their own copy or make notes on a separate piece of paper (visual notes such as small pictures or diagrams can be encouraged as well as written notes). Claire Taylor again describes her use of this technique:

> To extend our work on note taking and to prevent them copying the text directly, I read the text to them and they made notes. This also supported the less fluent reader, who might have less non-fiction experience and also gave me an opportunity to assess their listening skills. We discussed as a class what they had heard and compared notes. This task was obviously difficult and certain children had struggled. Again to demonstrate the skills involved, a child then read the text to me and I made notes on the shared writing board. We discussed the speed required, abbreviations and the lack of neatness. My notes were then available for all to refer to so no-one was excluded from the final task of writing a paragraph under each of the headings they had decided on.

Playing the 'Notes Game'

Teachers can also refine children's note taking skills by playing the 'Notes Game' in those few minutes before the children go out to play, etc. In this game the teacher writes a sentence from a current topic book on the board. One teacher used the sentence, 'The skill of Roman builders can be seen in the remains we have of roads, villas, baths, public buildings and city walls.' The teacher then asks the children, 'Who can give me this information in the fewest possible words?' If a child offers, 'The Romans were good builders', the teacher writes this on the board and asks 'Do we need *the*? Any other suggestions? Anything else we don't need?' Finally an agreed note is arrived at. 'Roman builders good. Evidence – remains' was what the children finally decided on for the above sentence. Children seem to enjoy these quick note taking practice games and are then encouraged to use the same strategy in their own note taking.

TELLING SOMEONE ELSE WHAT YOU HAVE LEARNT

When our pupils have finished a piece of research we often wish them to communicate the results in some way, for this not only provides a record of the children's work but is in itself a part of the learning process. In writing about or telling others about our ideas we clarify these for ourselves. This is a common experience for teachers, many of whom find that when explaining something to their pupils for the first time, for example, fractions, or electricity, they begin to understand that subject more clearly themselves – the act of communication helps clarify ideas. This does suggest that giving children plenty of opportunities to discuss ideas with their peers and to explain things to other people, in oral or written form, should be a fairly high priority in our classrooms.

The major way in which we ask children to communicate what they have found out through research is in writing and we will consider writing in a range of non-fiction genres in a subsequent chapter. There are, however, other ways in which children might communicate what they have learnt.

Oral presentations

There are many ways in which our pupils can communicate orally what it is they have learnt and most of these will be familiar to teachers as they are widely used. Here are just a few suggestions:

- drama, improvised or scripted, using the researched information as a basis. As an example, one class concluded their project on Columbus by collaboratively writing and then acting out a short play telling the events in his journey to the New World.
- making a radio programme. One class had been researching life in other countries and produced a tape-recorded travel documentary complete with contributions from several budding Alan Whickers.
- producing a class assembly. One class presented their work on frogs to the rest of the school in assembly and included readings from the books they had written, overhead transparencies and even extracts from a computer-based magazine they had produced on the subject.

Other popular and effective strategies include situations where children are questioned on what they have learnt. Such activities are often called 'the expert's chair' or 'hot seating' and usually involve certain rituals – the child sits on a special experts' chair or holds a 'book of knowledge' or wears a special item of clothing or badge of office.

They sit in front of their audience (the rest of the class, children from other classes, etc.) and invite questions from the audience on their area of research. This can be a straightforward question and answer session or the activity can be extended further by the children under question being required to answer in 'role', e.g. as Victorian children rather than as a themselves. The children usually enjoy such sessions immensely and their effectiveness both as a means of communicating what has been learnt, as well as providing a purpose for the research task, is clear.

Book making

The role of book making and publishing children's own work is a well established practice in relation to children writing stories and there are plenty

(a)

Figure 8.2 (a), (b) and (c) Front cover, sample page and contents page of a non-fiction book made by Year 1 children

Dangerous things for snails.

A snail curls up in its shell to hide from danger.
Hedgehogs and badgers eat snails.
Some people like to eat snails.
Thrushes and other birds like to eat snails. The thrush bangs the shell on a stone to break it.

(b)

of sources of advice on how to do it (see, for example, Johnson, 1994). Most teachers are very well aware of the motivational effects of such a practice and the purpose it gives to the writing. Book making also promotes knowledge about books and an understanding of how they are organised.

The same arguments also apply with regard to children producing non-fiction books. By this we do not mean the common practice of saving all the child's pieces of topic work and then sticking them together in a book. Rather we mean the planned non-fiction book, on a specific topic, which takes into account not only the content of the book but also the features of non-fiction books such as a glossary, index, contents page, etc. Many of the teachers we have worked with have undertaken book making with their pupils as a

Contents

(c)

purposeful way of communicating information. Figure 8.2 shows extracts from one such book produced by Key Stage 1 children. The book contains a contents page, an index and a glossary as well as the information they had researched. On completion it became a much admired addition to the class library.

This was just one of several non-fiction books produced by children in a first school in Doncaster and the child authors were able to witness their act of communication being used and admired each day as other children read their book. The full account of how such young children were scaffolded through the processes involved in researching information and producing such excellent products would require too much space, so for the present we will restrict ourselves to describing in detail how the teacher supported one group of children in making an index for their book.

Once their text had been researched and written, under a series of chapter headings such as, *What do snails look like?*, *What do snails eat?*, etc., a copy of the text was printed off (it had been word processed by the children and then corrected). The children went through the text underlining the key words in each sentence (see Figure 8.3).

These key words were typed into a list and cut up into individual words. The teacher then provided an alphabet grid and the words were copied out under the appropriate letter (see Figure 8.4).

Having organised an alphabetical list of the key words the children then went back to their dummy manuscript and noted down the page numbers alongside each word on the alphabetical list. Now they had their index (see Figure 8.5).

Older children would need less support than these 5 and 6 year olds but in creating their own index the children became acutely aware of the function and usefulness of an index and can often be seen sitting in their book corner sharing indexes with each other!

Dangerous things for snails

A snail curls up in its shell to hide from danger.
Hedgehogs and badgers eat snails.
Some people like to eat snails.
Thrushes and other birds like to eat snails. The thrush
bangs the shell on a stone to break it.

Figure 8.3 Making an index – a dummy page with the key words underlined

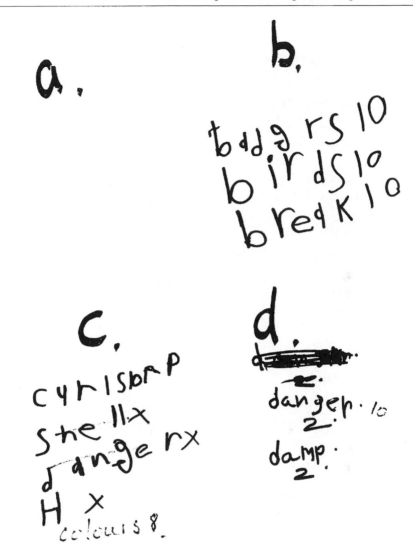

Figure 8.4 Making an index – adding key words to an ABC chart

Index

badgers 10
birds 10
break 10

colours 8
curls 10

damp 2
danger 2,10

eggs 4
eyes 8

foot 4

ground 2

hedgehogs 10
home 2
horns 8

live 2

people 10
plants 4
protect 8

shell 2,8,10
slide 4
slime 4
slither 4
stones 8,10

thrushes 10

upside down 4

Figure 8.5 Completed index

Chapter 9

A look at critical reading

TEXTS TO PERSUADE

During 1994 and 1995 the telephone company, Mercury, ran a series of advertisements for its services which probably affected teachers rather differently than other members of the population. Each advertisement was designed to look like two pages from a book, the right hand page containing a drawn picture and the left hand several lines of text in large bold print. The pictures always featured a family of father, mother, one male and one female child, plus, usually, a dog, engaged in family pursuits such as going for a ride in a car, or picking blackberries. The father always wore a blue pin-striped suit (he was modelled on the comedian Harry Enfield, a regular in Mercury advertisements), the mother a floral print dress. The accompanying text was written in a series of very short sentences, extolling the father's selection of Mercury as his telephone company, such as 'Well done, Daddy!' Underneath the main text, in smaller print, was a series of what were labelled 'Key words' which in reality made up an advertising slogan, such as 'Mercury twenty five per cent less'.

Most readers of this book, being teachers, will instantly recognise the form of such advertisements and something inside them will say 'Reading scheme'. The format of the two pages, one picture, one text; the content of the 'story' being told; the nature of the language used; the presence of the key words: all these features will instantly recall a reading scheme very popular in schools during the 1960s and 70s – the Ladybird Keywords reading scheme – on which many, many contemporary adults learned to read. For non-teacher adults, these advertisements will evoke a pleasant nostalgia for the carefree days of their own childhoods and the subliminal message will be conveyed that, if only they were to use the Mercury telephone system, things might once again be that carefree.

But, of course, this is an advertisement we are discussing. The whole point of advertisements is to persuade their readers to buy a particular product or act in a particular way. It has to be part of the job of the teacher of literacy to evoke in pupils the propensity to be critical with regard to these texts, and many others. It would hardly do if readers went around believing absolutely everything they saw in print: this would leave them open to the most blatant propaganda and biased text, of which advertisements are only one form. Yet what does it mean to be a critical reader, and how might teachers develop this ability in their pupils?

WHAT DOES IT MEAN TO BE A CRITICAL READER?

We deliberately chose the example of the Mercury advertisement because, as an audience consisting largely of teachers, you are probably already adopting a fairly critical stance to this text. Because you are familiar with the texts to which it relates (or their more recent equivalents) you can stand back from this advertisement and read in a sceptical way. (Our guess is that this campaign had little effect upon teachers because of the 'baggage' most of them were able to bring to its reading.) What you are able to do quite consciously is to place this particular example of language use firmly into its social context. It is this which seems to be at the heart of critical reading.

By being explicitly aware of the social context of this text you are able to consider such questions as:

- Why has the author used this particular language?
- Why have the advertisers chosen this picture?
- Why have they used this layout?

These questions imply a recognition that in the production of any text there are always alternative possibilities which the author has rejected for some reason. A consideration of what those alternatives were and why they were rejected by the author can bring us closer to an understanding of what the author's intentions were for this text. Understanding those intentions allows us to reject them if we so wish.

The fact is that all texts are located in a particular set of social practices and understandings. They involve choices. Critical reading involves an explicit examination of these choices and hence the particular social understandings and values underlying texts.

THE ROLES OF THE READER

It is useful at this point to draw upon the descriptive framework of reader roles proposed by Freebody and Luke (1990). They suggest that to be a successful reader in current society involves developing the ability to function in four related reader roles:

a) a code-breaker (How can I crack this? What does it say?)
b) a text participant (How can I understand this? What does this mean?)
c) a text user (How can I use this? What can I do with it?)
d) a text analyst (How can I respond to this? What does this do to me?)

Becoming aware of what a text does to you demands an awareness of where it has come from and why it is as it is. There are several key questions which follow from such an awareness:

* Who produced this text?
* What is its purpose?
* What choices were made during its production?
* Why were these choices made?

This view depends upon an understanding that text is not the transparent conveyor of meaning it is sometimes thought to be. Rather it is a constructed entity. Some*body* writes texts and some*body* reads them. Both those bodies make choices, conscious or unconscious, about the ways they construct a text, which means that the acts of reading and writing are a good deal less precise than we often think. An example may make this clearer.

A text which has achieved a considerable popularity in this country is the Australian TV soap opera 'Neighbours' (this is a media text but similar rules apply as with any text, printed or otherwise). This text purports to show daily life in a typical Australian suburban community. Australians of our acquaintance, however, find this notion very amusing and claim not to recognise 'Neighbours' as typically Australian at all. What has happened is that the authors of this text have selected parts of the Australian life style to represent in the TV programme – and, therefore, rejected others. Why have they done this and on what basis have they made their choices?

Now when some people (often teenagers for some reason) watch 'Neighbours' they becomes absorbed in the plot lines, identify with the characters and express the desire to go to live in Australia. For them the choice is to accept this representation as, at least partially, true to real life. Other people (wiser older heads like us!) read this text very differently, if we read it at all. For us it is not meant to approximate to real life but is no more than a caricature. The characters and plot lines therefore become humorous and we watch it for a little light relief and 'a bit of a laugh'. Here then both writers and readers of this text have made choices about the ways they will represent the meanings the text deals with.

LANGUAGE CONSTRUCTS OUR WORLD

The constructive and selective nature of both reading and writing would be no problem to us if it were always as conscious a process as the example above suggests. Unfortunately, much of the decision-making which goes on as we respond to texts we read takes place at an unconscious or subconscious level. This means that we are not always aware of the effects the language of texts is having upon us. And it does have an incredibly powerful effect, even to the extent of almost totally constructing our view of parts of the world, much of which we only ever have access to through the texts which represent it.

The power of language in our construction of language is well seen in the following example. During the 1992 Gulf War with Iraq the British press and media were, to most people, the only ways in which news of the conflict could be obtained. The ways in which that conflict was described had some very interesting features as shown in the following list.

Expressions used in the British Press during the Gulf War

We have:	*They have:*
Army, Navy and Airforce	A war machine
Reporting guidelines	Censorship
Press briefings	Propaganda

We:	*They:*
Take out	Kill
Suppress	Destroy

Our men are:	*Their men are:*
Boys	Troops
Lads	Hordes
Cautious	Cowardly
Confident	Desperate
Loyal	Blindly obedient
Brave	Fanatical

Our planes:	*Their planes:*
Fail to return from missions	Are shot out of the sky

Most liberal-minded people would, perhaps, claim that this biased use of language had little effect upon them. It is, however, its very pervasiveness and the fact that it is so rarely questioned which is its most worrying feature.

Here is another example which will be even clearer in its implications. The following description of the Battle of Vegkop, in 1836, is taken from the 1980 official South African primary history textbook:

> The trekkers hurried into the laager and closed the entrance. All around were the Matabele hordes, sharpening their assegais, killing animals and drinking the raw blood. Sarel Celliers offered up a prayer.
>
> When the enemy made a savage attack, the defenders fired volley upon volley into their ranks. All helped. The women and children loaded extra guns and handed them to the men. After a fierce battle, the Matabele fled with their tails between their legs. The voortrekkers gave thanks to God for their deliverance.

The following account of the same event was published in the 1988 Reader's Digest *Illustrated History of South Africa*.

The trekkers' first major confrontation was with Mzilikazi, founder and king of the Ndebele. In 1836 the Ndebele were in the path of a trekker expedition heading northwards. . . . The Ndebele were attacked by a Boer commando but Mzilikazi retaliated and the Boers retreated to their main laager at Vegkop. There, after a short and fierce battle, 40 trekkers, thanks to their guns and an efficient reloading system, succeeded in beating off an attack by 6000 Ndebele warriors. 400 Ndebele were killed and the trekkers' sheep and cattle herds were virtually annihilated.

Contrasting these accounts raises several important questions:

- Who first attacked whom in this battle? The implication in the textbook account is that the battle was caused by the 'Matabele hordes' whereas the second account has it that the Boers attacked first simply because the Ndbele were in their way.
- Who won the battle? In one account the Matabele 'fled with their tails between their legs' whereas in the other they were beaten off but succeeded in killing all the Boers' livestock, which presumably meant that there was no way in which the Boers could now survive in an inhospitable landscape.
- What are the effects of the particular choices of language made by both authors? The tribespeople are variously referred to as 'Matabele' and 'Ndbele'. Which of these names is most likely to have been their name for themselves? What are the effects of language such as 'drinking the raw blood' and 'a savage attack'?

This example reminds us that the term 'bias' is one we use to refer to the presentation of ideas we do not agree with. In fact, by definition, all texts are biased since they all involve choices of words and structures stemming from the view of the world held by their authors. These texts in turn construct the world for readers.

TEXTS IN SCHOOL

The construction of readers' worlds by texts is just as true of school texts as it is of out of school texts. Baker and Freebody's (1989) research into children's first school books revealed some interesting features of these texts and their effects.

Classrooms are places where children learn about their worlds through socially-approved texts

It is a fact that only certain texts are given a place in classrooms. There is a heavy emphasis on:

- book texts. Non-book texts actually take up far more of adult reading time but in classrooms the book reigns supreme. Some non-book texts are occasionally given a place. Some teachers, for example, allow their children to read comics, although by no means all (Wray and Lewis, 1993). Even when comics are allowed, however, they are restricted to those which are socially approved. Few teachers will allow comics such as *Viz*, for example.
- particular genres. Narrative predominates both in reading and writing. Coming from the kinds of print-rich worlds that they do, it is quite likely that young children arrive at school with a roughly equal familiarity with narrative and non-narrative texts. Out of school they encounter print used for a wide range of purposes (Heath, 1983), but early on in their school careers they learn that narrative is more highly approved and begin to act accordingly.
- improving texts. Many texts in school are chosen because of their moral messages. Children tend not to be introduced to texts in which the protagonists despair, murder, commit suicide, rape. They are much more likely to meet characters who overcome difficulties or are rewarded for good actions.

Children learn the texts' versions of what it means to be children (including what it means to be male and female)

This is, of course, well worn ground and we are all familiar now with critiques of the -isms in children's books (racism, sexism and classism). Although there are still points to take note of in this area of debate, it is probably true that the gross excesses of previous generations' children's books, especially reading schemes (for example, the scheme pastiched by the Mercury advertisement with which we began this chapter), are a thing of the past in these more enlightened, politically correct days. Yet there are still images of childhood implicit in the texts which children are given in schools. There are certain things that children do and do not do in books for children. As Baker and Freebody (1989) put it:

> Children's first school books, in explicit and implicit ways, propound a version of childhood – in effect a theory of how children think, act and talk, and of their position in the social world. This invites, and possibly requires, children to revise their own identities at least for purposes of successfully engaging in school reading instruction and in using the discourse of the books to talk (indirectly) about themselves.

(p. 152)

Children learn how success at reading and writing is defined by their teachers

Adam is a bright little boy, now 6 years old and thriving at school. He had been read to regularly from a very young age and shared a lively imaginative world with such characters as Mr Gumpy, Max and the wild things, Peter Rabbit and so on. When invited to read he had no hesitation in accepting and sharing a favourite book with whoever would join in. After two months at school, however, his definition of reading changed remarkably. He now read only out loud and accompanied this by stabbing a finger irregularly at words on the page. When invited to read, he would often reply 'I can't read that yet'. 'Reading' for Adam was now really concerned with learning to say the words that came home with him in his tin.

This kind of change in children is, unfortunately, often observed and begs the question of whether the definition of success at reading which they seem to learn very quickly in school is really such a helpful one.

The picture is similar in writing. Many children learn very quickly at school that they cannot write, undoing the confidence in mark-making which they often bring with them. For others what counts as writing changes subtly. Looking at the writing in figure 9.1, most readers will be able to hazard a fairly good guess as to where this child has learnt what counts as successful writing.

TEACHING CRITICAL READERS: CLASSROOM STRATEGIES

Bearing in mind the points raised above about the nature of critical reading, there are several approaches to classroom work which seem promising.

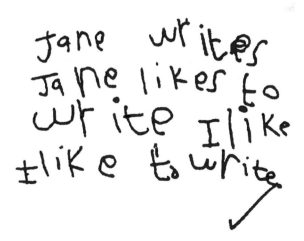

Figure 9.1 Early successful writing?

Encourage discussion of texts

This discussion should centre not just around what texts mean, but should also concern their purpose and the choices made in their production. Questions to guide this discussion might include:

- Who produced this text?
  What are his/her qualifications for doing so?
- What is its purpose?
  Does the author tell you what the purpose is?
  Is there a hidden purpose?
- What choices were made during its production?
  What formats, structures, vocabulary were rejected?
- Why were these choices made?
  What would be different if different choices had been made?

Such questions might seem difficult, but there is evidence from an emerging literature that even quite young children are capable of discussing them if the context is right. Jennifer O'Brien (1994a), for example, describes how, after reading Roald Dahl's *The Fantastic Mr Fox* to a class of six year olds, she asked them the following question:

> In this story Roald Dahl shows Mrs Fox to be weak and scared. Draw a different Mrs Fox helping to save her family. Use speech bubbles and labels to show what she could say and do to save her family.
>
> (p. 38)

The children drew pictures of a strong and adventurous Mrs Fox planning and digging to save her family. O'Brien gives several examples of this nature and, in another article (O'Brien, 1994b) describes how she engaged 5 to 7 year olds in looking critically at Mother's Day catalogues to discuss the idealised pictures of mothers portrayed in these catalogues. She asked these children to produce alternative catalogues giving a different picture of mothers. This idea of children writing new versions of texts making different choices seems to have plenty of possibilities.

It is also quite possible now, of course, for children to examine different versions of the same story and talk about why changes have been made. They might, for example, compare Jon Scieska's *The True Story of the Three Little Pigs* with traditional version(s) of that story. There are plenty of examples of such 'fractured fairy tales' to choose from.

Confront children with texts which arise from different viewpoints about the world

This can happen quite naturally during classroom work. One group of nine year olds, for example, while working on a project on space came across a dispute in the books they were reading. In one book it told them that Saturn had 15 moons: in another they were told it had 16 moons. At first the children simply wanted to know which of these books was telling the truth and which was 'lying'. In fact, the picture was found to be more complex. When the dates of publication of the two books were examined it was found that there was about a ten year gap. The teacher and the children reasoned, therefore, that in that ten year period scientists had probably discovered a fresh moon around Saturn (according to the latest information available, Saturn now has probably 22 moons. See the World Wide Web, http://bang.lanl.gov/solarsys/satnew.htm).

The fact that information does not remain static but is ever changing is an important understanding for children. It can be introduced to them deliberately by contrasting older and newer books on a similar subject. Compare, for example, books about computers published more than about fifteen years ago with the latest volumes. In one source, computers fill rooms and store data on large, whirling tapes: in another they fit on desks and in pockets and store data on small square 'discs' or objects like credit cards.

There are other areas in which texts can be found which contradict each other. A class of eight year olds were studying the Norman invasion of Britain in 1066. They had been given access to translated accounts of the invasion written by Norman and also by Anglo-saxon chroniclers and were fascinated to compare such accounts, which told radically different stories. Their teacher's response to the inevitable question, 'Who's telling the truth?' was to explain that, in all probability, nobody was. The nature of historical records is such that it is almost impossible for there not to be a 'point of view' in the writing. As any Black South African, American Indian, or even Scot, will testify, what counts as history is almost always told from the point of view of the victors. Children need to be introduced to this idea by studying contrasting texts.

An easy way into this area is to use newspaper reports about the same events from different newspapers. The approach of a newspaper such as the *Daily Telegraph* is very different from that of the *Guardian*, and different again from that of the *Sun*. Children can gain a great deal by looking carefully at newspapers like these and comparing their treatment of a story, the points they emphasise, the language they use and the pictures and headlines they employ to highlight the story.

Encourage children to produce their own texts for a range of socially important purposes

We have stressed earlier in this book the importance of authentic activities for children's learning. Given these activities many children will actually want to write to achieve purposes which matter to them. Examples of this range from children writing to the local council to complain about the litter in the streets around the school to children writing to their headteacher arguing that they should be allowed to eat snacks in the school playground. This last example reminds us that such authentic writing does not necessarily have to relate to out-of-school activities. Purposes which are real to children tend to come from their own social worlds – which includes school. As an example, the writing in Figure 9.2, was undoubtedly authentic for the child who wrote it, and suggests a great deal about the context for literacy the teacher had created in that classroom.

Give children access to the socially agreed forms used in texts written for different purposes

This approach will be explored in much greater detail in the following chapter in which we will discuss our approach to structuring children's non-fiction writing through writing frames. The key to this approach is that particular writing forms and structures have emerged to meet particular communication purposes. We have found it possible to introduce children to these structures through the scaffold of writing frames.

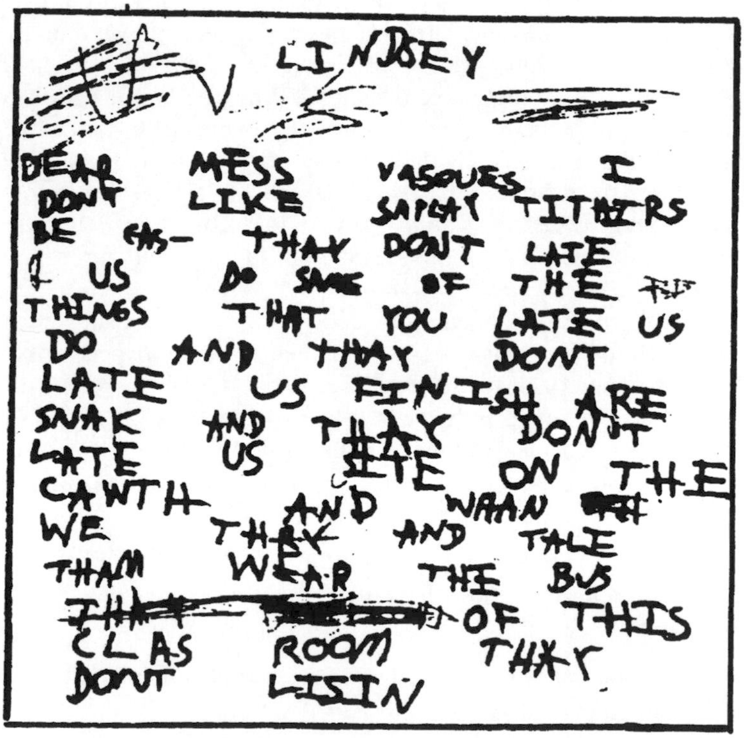
LINDSEY
DEAR MESS VASQUES I DONT LIKE SAPLAY TITHERS BE CAS- THAY DONT LATE US DO SAME OF THE THINGS THAT YOU LATE US DO AND THAY DONT LATE US FINISH ARE SNAK AND THAY DONT LATE US ETE ON THE CAWTH AND WAAN WE TH AND TALE THAM WEAR THE BUS OF THIS CLAS ROOM THAY DONT LISIN

Figure 9.2 Writing a complaint

FINAL POINT

It is very important to see a critical approach to literacy as being part of literacy teaching from the very beginning. We cannot teach literacy, then teach children to be critical. A critical approach is part of what we define as literacy in the modern world and needs to be part of our teaching from the very beginning. We have found in our work no support at all for the argumen that young children are 'not ready' for this approach. After all, by the time the vast majority of them arrive at school, they are already very critical readers of other kinds of texts. School needs to build on this.

Chapter 10

Writing non-fiction

At the end of Chapter 8 we discussed some of the ways that children might communicate what they had discovered about a subject, whilst the many forms of text remodelling we discussed in Chapter 7 also provide ways of communicating what we have learnt. However a major way of communicating in the classroom remains that of writing about a topic and it is to non-fiction writing that we now wish to turn.

Perhaps the most common way we ask children to communicate their research results is by asking them to write about it. Here is a brief extract from Gary's two page writing up of his research into the Spanish Armada.

His opening makes it clear that to Gary this is an exciting story and it ends with a suitably dramatic climax when the enemy have 'their brains split'. Although this might be an exciting story, as a vehicle for communicating the facts it is unsatisfactory – the causes of the battle, the sequence of events and the relationship of the participants are not clear and yet Gary is obviously engaged by the battle, its preparation and conclusion. What we see in Gary's writing is how the genre he has chosen to use (narrative recount) has not supported him in his attempts to clarify the why and what of the Armada. A clearly sectioned report with subheadings such as 'What were the causes of the quarrel?', 'Who took part', 'The early stages of the battle', 'How the Armada ended' may have helped Gary plan his writing more clearly and write it up in a more coherent way. On this occasion Gary had undertaken some reading and had then been asked to 'write about it'. This kind of writing request often prompts some kind of recount of what has been done/read and teachers need to be aware when requesting a writing outcome that they need to signal a range of writing to children. Asking children to 'explain' or 'describe' or 'discuss' or 'tell me about' all invite different kinds of writing response.

Making the purpose of the writing clear is important as different purposes are likely to give rise to different types of writing. Figure 10.2 summarises the main purposes of non-fiction writing and the kind of writing that would arise. However, simply making sure the purpose is explicit and signalling the type of writing by the way we word the writing task is not in itself enough. Even

A Long time ago in 1588 King philip
II Wanted to inVacle England.
Suddenly aletter came From
The Netherlands and it said "I'm sorry
but I'm Not going to Fight you
because iF Feel sick." So The Gental
Said NoNe of them are coming to
Fight US and So it Looks Like
Just us and England This time.
But in Spain They Were building
avery big Ship called The armada,
When They had builte It They had
130 ship in Side The armada had
8,000 Sailors and 20,000 Soldiers and
180 priests to Make people cathlic
again. They also had guns
Medical equipment Food Water gun
powder and Canons all in The armada
and They had Slaves to pull The
armada into The sea.
                    But back in
England They had Ships readey and
They had Food & Water and Nearly all
of The armey. Then They Set Sail

The Spainish Lost Nearly all his Men
and Some was danding and Some
Was hanged and Some came to Shore
in Scotlen and when They did
The Scottish got brikes and They
smashed The Spainishies heads until
their brains split.

Figure 10.1 Writing about the Armada

Purpose of writing	Generic form
• to retell events with the purpose of either informing or entertaining	recount
• to describe the way things are	report
• to explain the processes involved in natural and social phenomena, or to explain how something works	explanation
• to describe how something is done through a series of sequenced steps	procedure
• to promote a particular point of view or argument	persuasive
• to present arguments and information from differing viewpoints before reaching a conclusion based on the evidence	discussion

Figure 10.2 Purposes for writing and their generic form

if the purpose for writing is clear, children may still continue to write recounts when another form of writing might help them achieve their purpose more effectively. Kim's writing (Figure 10.3) is a very good example of this. Having planted some cress seeds in class Kim, a confident language user, had made her own packet of cress seeds in order to take some seeds home to sow. She had looked at some examples of seed packets and discussed the kind of information that was written on the back of these and the ways in which it was written. However, on her own packet she wrote a straightforward recount of the planting activity she had just completed. The inclusion of other factual information shows she had studied the backs of the seeds packets carefully but she had not adopted the most appropriate written form for conveying sowing instructions.

In this case Kim had been asked to write the instructions she would need to follow when she took the seeds home. It would seem that Kim had failed to recognise the appropriate generic form (procedural) that would have made her writing more effective in achieving its aim of giving directions for planting. She is not alone in this. Most teachers will recognise occasions when children write a recount of what they did rather than offer an explanation or give instructions or write a report. This response springs from the well established, well understood and important tradition of offering children 'real experiences' and then asking them to write about them. Such a request invites a personal telling. It is of course very important that children write in this way but we also need to encourage children to move from always giving a personal recount to the more formal and abstract writing demanded to write a report, an explanation, a procedure, an argument and a discussion. In order to do this we need first to understand something about the way different non-fiction texts are structured in order that we may share this understanding with our pupils.

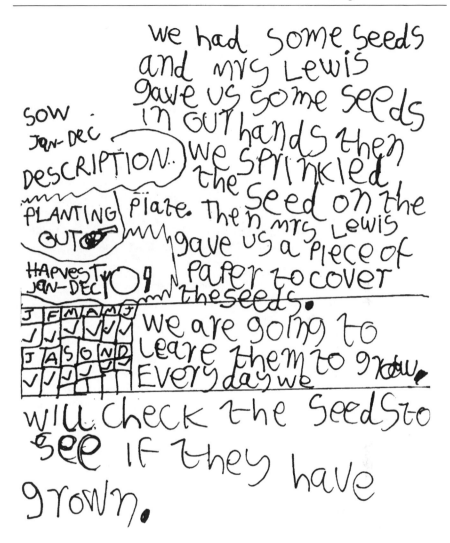

Figure 10.3 Kim's seed packet instructions
(We had some seeds and Mrs Lewis gave us some seeds in our hands then we
sprinkled the seeds on the plate. Then Mrs Lewis gave us a piece of paper to cover
the seeds. We are going to leave them to grow. Everyday we will check the seeds
to see if they have grown.)

THE STRUCTURES OF THE MAIN NON-FICTION WRITTEN GENRES

Recent work, mainly from Australia (e.g. Kress and Knapp, 1992; Martin and
Rothery, 1986) and taken up in the UK (Lewis and Wray, 1995; Littlefair,

1991), has looked at the generic structures of non-fiction written forms. Discussing the generic structures of some types of writing is well established in our classrooms. We are all familiar with the idea that stories have a general shape. Most fairy stories, for example, follow the structure of:

opening, setting the scene;
events, often in the form of problems/resolutions or meetings/consequences;
ending.

All readers are implicitly aware of this structure and increasingly teachers may decide to make it explicit to their pupils in order to help them plan and write such a story. A great deal of work has been done what is often called story grammar (e.g. Mandler and Johnson, 1977). The structures of non-fiction texts can also be broadly identified (Derewianka, 1990). For example a procedural text (a 'how to' text such as a recipe, a set of instructions, etc.) has the structure:

Goal	How to make a book.
Materials and equipment	Sugar paper, card, needle and thread, glue.
Steps to take to achieve the goal	Fold the sugar paper in half to make the pages of the book. . . .

If we examine examples of such texts, or even consider how we give instructions to groups of children, we can see that procedural, 'how to', texts tend to follow this generic structure. The generic structures of non-fiction texts can all be broadly identified and Figure 10.4 shows the generic structure of the main types of non fiction writing.

There are of course many other kinds of non-fiction genres and many examples of mixed genre texts.

USING OUR KNOWLEDGE OF NON-FICTION GENERIC STRUCTURES TO SUPPORT CHILDREN'S WRITING

The most obvious way we can help children become familiar with the structures of non-fiction texts is by having, and using examples of such texts in our classrooms. We may for example have recipe books, books showing how to make puppets, fire instructions on the wall, rules of games, notices alongside the computer instructing how to load a program and so on. These are all procedural texts. Our classrooms need to contain the full range of non-fiction texts so that our children experience books, pamphlets, letters and documents of all kinds written in a variety of genres. We also need to read aloud to children from this wide range of non-fiction texts as well as fiction texts for we need to help them become familiar with the structures, patterns and rhythms of all texts. This 'immersion' is important. As Margaret Meek

• a 'scene setting' opening (orientation) e.g. *I went on a visit to the museum ...*	• an opening, general classification e.g. *Exeter is a city in Devon.*	• a statement of what is to be achieved (goal) e.g. *How to make a sponge cake.*
• a recount of the events as they occurred (events) e.g. *I sat with my friend on the bus...etc*	• a description of the phenomena, which includes some or all of its: – qualities e.g. *Exeter is situated on the river Exe.*	• a list of materials/ equipment needed to achieve the goal e.g. *2 eggs.*
• a closing statement (reorientation) e.g. *When we got back from the trip we wrote about it.*	– parts and their function *The city is the county town of Devon. It has the university, court...* – habits/behaviour or uses *County Hall is the administrative centre...*	• a series of sequenced steps to achieve the goal e.g. *Cream the sugar and butter.* • often there is a diagram or illustration

EXPLANATION	ARGUMENT	DISCUSSION
• a general statement to introduce the topic e.g. *A butterfly goes through several stages in its life cycle.* • a series of logical steps explaining how or why something occurs These steps continue until the final state is produced or the explanation is complete. e.g. *The adult butterfly lays eggs on a suitable leaf. The eggs hatch and a caterpillar emerges...*	• an opening statement (the thesis) – often in the form of position/ preview e.g. *Fox hunting should be banned for it is a cruel and barbaric sport.* • the arguments (often in the form of point + elaboration) e.g. *Foxes rarely attack domestic animals. Statistics show that ...* • a summary and restatement of the opening position (reiteration) e.g. *We have seen that... Therefore, all the evidence points to the conclusion... that fox hunting is clearly cruel and unnecessary.*	• a statement of the issue + a preview of the main arguments e.g. *Should we have school uniform? Individuality or group identity?* • arguments for + supporting evidence • arguments against + supporting evidence • recommendation given as a summary and conclusion e.g. *We have seen... I think that...*

Figure 10.4 A brief outline of the generic structures of some written forms

(Meek, 1988: p. 21) says, 'The most important single lesson the children learn from texts is the nature and variety of written discourse, the different ways that language lets a writer tell, and the many different ways a reader reads.'

We can then help our pupils make explicit their implicit knowledge based on familiarity with a range of text types. We may do this through teacher modelling and shared writing experiences. Together we may write up the procedural text that relates to others how we made our Tudor pomander or constructed our kite, etc. And as we write together we discuss the structure of the text and the language choices we make as we construct it.

TEACHER MODELLING/SHARED WRITING IN PRACTICE

Look at this procedural text (Figure 10.5) produced in a shared writing session.

After making a toy the group of children were writing up the instructions for the rest of the class to undertake the task. The teacher took the opportunity to model how to write a procedure. After working with the group to compose the title (goal) and the list of materials that were needed the teacher provided the first sentence of the instructions. This was in the imperative tense (see Figure 10.5). This provided a model of the register of the text and for the next step which the children were invited to provide. Two more steps were offered and written by the children, both maintaining the imperative, procedural form. At step 4, however, one child offered and then wrote, 'We folded each corner into the middle.' This child had slipped into recount genre. When this was written the teacher read through the whole piece of writing to the children and asked for their comments. Sasha said 'That's not the right kind of sentence.'

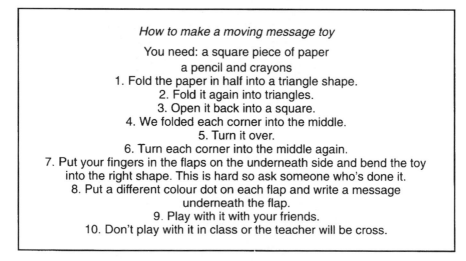

Figure 10.5 Procedural text produced during a shared writing session

The teacher asked the rest of the group if they agreed and if so what was wrong with it. They were able to point out that none of the other sentences contained the word 'we' and that all the 'right kind of sentences told you what to do'. The teacher then asked how sentence 4 could be made into the right kind of sentence. 'We' was crossed out and there was then a discussion as to whether the sentence was now 'right'. Changing 'folded' into 'fold' was soon suggested and the group was then happy that this sentence now conformed to the rest of the text. Notice how, in this example, the children had a reason for writing in this particular genre and the modelling of the form arose within the context of their ongoing work and normal writing practice within this class.

After several shared writing sessions using non-fiction written genres in this way many of the children begin to incorporate the genre into their independent writing. However, there may be those who continue to write recounts or write pieces that are for example a mixture of recount and procedure (see Figure 10.6).

This suggests that there are some children for whom further input is needed, something to span the shared activity and independent activity phase. We have called this additional input the scaffolded phase – a phase where we offer our pupils strategies to aid writing but strategies that they can use without an adult necessarily being alongside them. One such strategy is the use of writing frames.

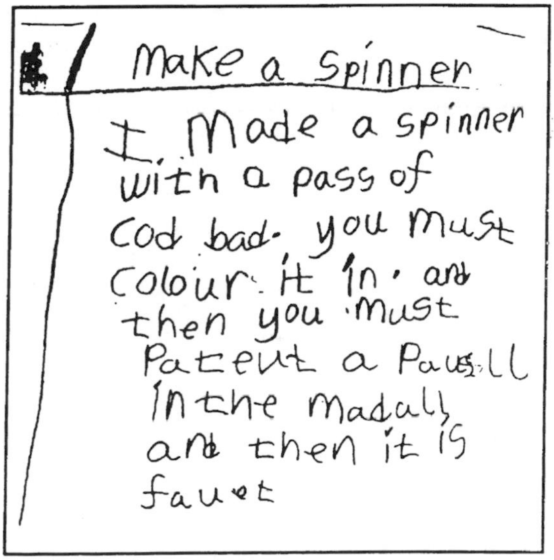
Make a Spinner
I made a spinner with a pass of Cod bad. you must colour it in. and then you must Pateut a Pausll in the madall and then it is fauet

Figure 10.6 Child's writing showing mixture of procedural and recount genre

WHAT ARE WRITING FRAMES?

A writing frame consists of a skeleton outline to scaffold and prompt children's non-fiction writing (see Figure 10.7).

The framework provides a 'template' of starters, connectives and sentence modifiers which gives children a structure within which they can concentrate on communicating what they want to say whilst scaffolding them in the use of a particular generic form. However, by using the form children also become increasingly familiar with it. Once the use of frames has been introduced using teacher modelling and shared writing it can also offer support when individual attention is not available and can continue to be used successfully by pupils within the normal classroom routines. Frames however do more than just scaffold generic structures.

HOW WRITING FRAMES CAN HELP

Cairney's (1990) work on story frames and Cudd and Roberts (1989) on 'expository paragraph frames' first suggested to us that some children, and especially those who were experiencing difficulties in writing, might find a written scaffold useful. Providing written structures to prompt writing seemed to mirror, but develop, the oral promptings that teachers have always instinctively offered to children. We have all worked alongside children offering supportive oral prompts such as 'And then?', 'What comes next?' and 'It looked like ...?', and in doing so we appear to be trying to span the gap between speech and written language which presents problems for some children. One reason often given for some of the difficulties which children experience in writing is that they are confused by these differences between

Although I already knew that

I have recently learnt some new information about
I have learnt that

I have also discovered that

I now know that

However, the most interesting thing I learnt was

Figure 10.7 A sample writing frame

the spoken and written forms. Bereiter and Scardamalia (1987) point out the supportive, prompting nature of conversation, for example, 'turn taking' – somebody speaks which prompts someone else to say something and so on. This reciprocal prompting is missing from the interaction between a writer and blank sheet of paper. Bereiter and Scardamalia's research has suggested that a teacher's oral promptings during writing can significantly extend a child's written work, with no drop in quality. The prompts act as an 'external trigger of discourse production' (1987, p. 97) and Bereiter and Scardamalia suggest that children need to 'acquire a functional substitute for ... an encouraging listener'. It seems that the written prompts provided by writing frames provide a step between the teacher's oral promptings and the child acquiring independence in writing.

Writing frames also help overcome other problems claimed for the writing of non-fiction texts. As well as a lack of knowledge of generic structures of non-fiction texts and the lack of prompting, others problems often mentioned are:

- the complexity of the cohesive ties children have to recognise and use,
- the use of more formal registers,
- the use of technical vocabulary.

(Derewianka, 1990; Littlefair, 1991.)

It appears that writing frames can help children overcome these problems by providing a framework that:

- helps maintain the cohesion of the whole,
- provides experience of appropriate connectives,
- models the more formal 'register' of non-fiction genres,
- introduces more complex vocabulary,
- scaffolds the appropriate generic form.

Other advantages of the frames commented on by the teachers who have used then are that they:

- enable children to achieve some success at writing, and in doing so,
- improve self esteem and motivation,
- prevent children from being presented with a blank sheet of paper – a daunting experience for some children who find starting a piece of writing difficult.

THE FRAMES IN USE

There are many possible writing frames for each of these six main non-fiction written forms (Lewis and Wray, 1995) and each make use of generic structures and varying connectives to help maintain the generic shape and cohesive sense of the whole piece of writing.

The use of a frame should always begin with discussion and teacher modelling before moving on to joint construction (teacher and child/ren together) and then to the child undertaking independent writing, supported by the frame. It is useful to make 'big' versions of the frames, using flip charts or overhead projector transparencies, for use in the teacher modelling and joint construction phases. During the shared writing, with sometimes the teacher and sometimes the child acting as scribe, it is important to demonstrate that the frame is a supportive draft and words may be crossed out or substituted. Extra sentences may be added or surplus starters crossed out. The frame should be treated as a flexible aid not a rigid form. This teacher modelling (i.e. teacher scribing and talking about what is being written and why) and joint construction pattern of teaching is an important first step for it not only models the generic form and teaches the words that signal connections and transitions in writing but also provides opportunities for developing children's oral language and thinking. Some children, especially those with learning difficulties, may need many oral sessions and sessions in which their teacher acts as a scribe before they are ready to attempt their own framed writing. Prior familiarity with the frame gives children the confidence to use them on their own.

It is also important to vary the wording of the prompts, for example a discussion may open with,

'The issue we are discussing is whether . . .', or
'Our class have been arguing about . . .', or
'There is a lot of comment in the news recently concerning . . .', or
'People have strong views about . . .'.

This changing of the prompts helps avoid the problem that the writing may become too formulaic. With some special needs children and reluctant writers, however, teachers may decide to stay with a familiar set of prompts for some time as for these children the repetition of phrases may be helpful to them.

PLANNING AND DRAFTING

As with all writing, framed writing should involve planning and drafting stages. Indeed the planning stage is vital in helping children marshal their ideas. In preparing to write a piece of persuasive writing the children can be encouraged to gather their arguments as a series of 'protest posters' (see Figure 10.8). These can also be developed into full size posters for part of the writing display for it helps remind children of the process they went through in order to reach their finished piece of writing.

Discussions can be planned by listing opposing arguments (see Figure 10.9), reports by gathering information in characteristics grids (see Figure 10.10) and so on.

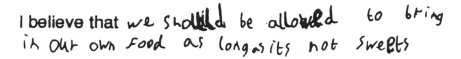

Write statements in the 'protest posters' to support your point of view.

Figure 10.8 Planning for writing an argument (food at breaktime)

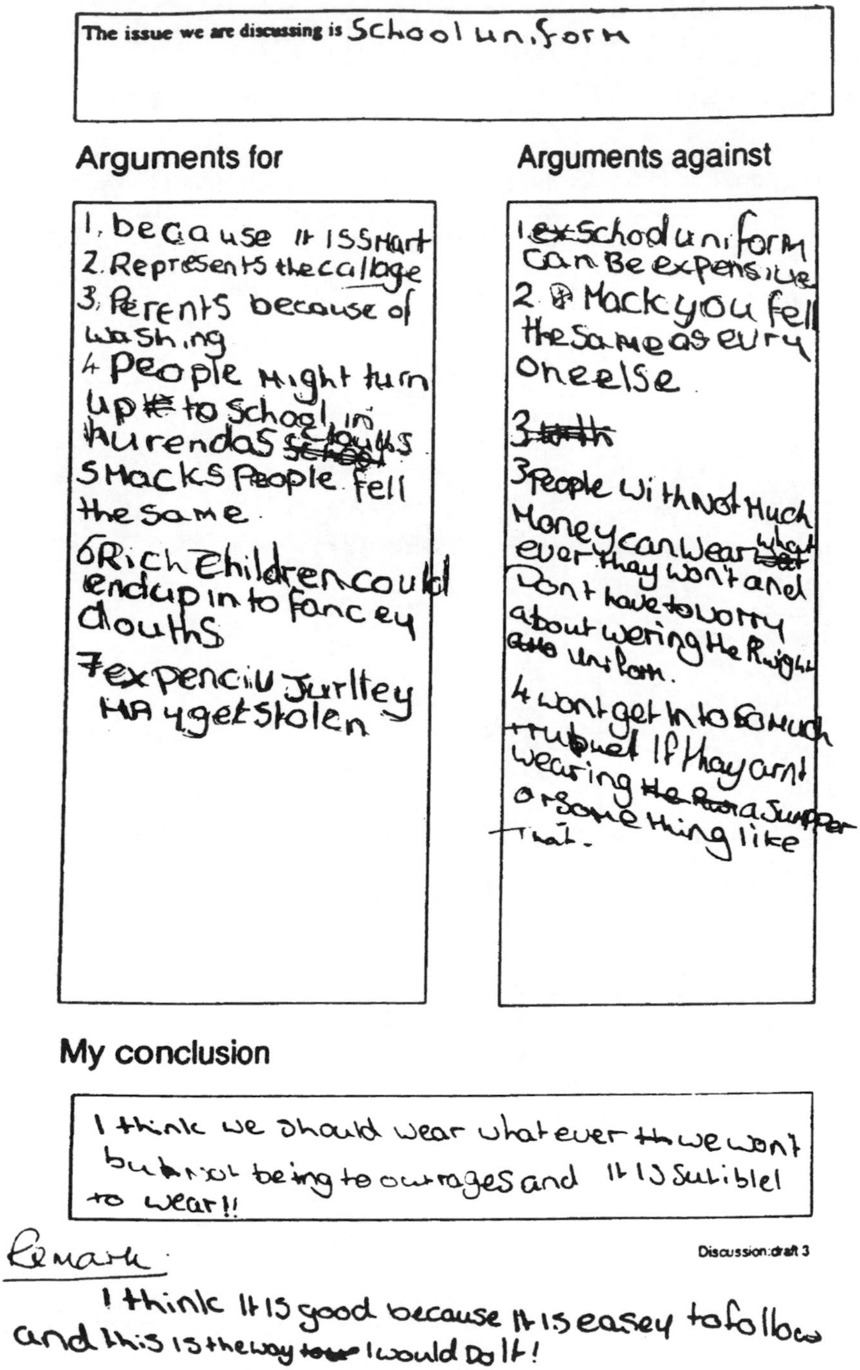

The issue we are discussing is School uniform

Arguments for

1. beCause It IS Smart
2. Represents the callage
3. Perents becouse of washing
4 People might turn up to School in hurendas clouths
5 Macks People fell the same.
6 Rich children could end up in to fancey clouths
7 expenciv Jurltey MA y get stolen

Arguments against

1 ex Schod uniform Can Be expensive
2 Mack you fell the Same as evry one else.
3
3 People with Not Much Money can wear what ever thay won't and Don't have to worry about wering the Right unifom.
4 wont get In to so much trubuel If thay arnt wearing the Poor a Jumper or something like That.

My conclusion

I think we should wear whatever we wont but not being to outrages and It IS Sutiblel to wear!!

Remark:

I think It IS good because It IS easey to follow and this is the way I would Do It!

Discussion:draft 3

Figure 10.9 Planning for writing a discussion (school uniform)

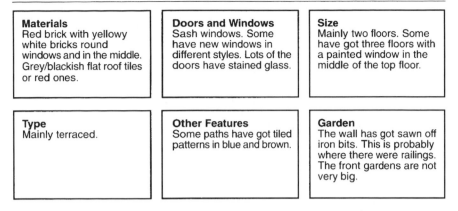

Figure 10.10 Planning for writing a report – listing of characteristics (Victorian houses)

Having undertaken the planning stage the frame is then used for a first draft (see Figure 10.11) and can then be used as the basis for a teacher/pupil conference, for pupil self editing or peer editing before a final piece is produced.

USING FRAMES WITH CHILDREN WITH LITERACY PROBLEMS

Figure 10.12 shows the use of an explanation frame by a child who receives individual literacy support for a few hours a week. Asking children with learning difficulties to write explanations is to set them a difficult task. Not only is the form unfamiliar but their response needs to be structured in a logical way. The inability to organise writing into logical or sequential steps often leads children to produce incoherent explanations. The format of the frames demands that they think before they write and offers them support in how to organise their ideas.

Prior knowledge frames, a form of recount genre (see Figure 10.13), are often the most successful way of introducing the frames to children experiencing writing difficulties as they build on a form they are already familiar with (recount). The 'starter phrase' prior knowledge frames offer the child the opportunity to display what they already know about a topic, thus giving them an immediate and successful way in to their writing. Through the use of the personalised sentence structure the child is an active participant in the writing, using their own voice. For example, one group of children with special needs had watched a video with their class on 'Life in Tudor and Stuart Times' and were then asked to write about what they had seen. What they would normally have produced, and then only after a great deal of coaxing and encouragement, would almost certainly have been only a few sentences recounting some of the video. On this occasion their support teacher used a

There is a lot of discussion about whether
■ cantona has had ~~in ther~~ punishment ✓
~~enough~~

The people who agree with this idea, such as -David
claim that The man that called cantona
names ~~dezerved~~ ~~to~~ being kicked punche
and ~~who~~ ~~coat~~ what ever.

They also argue that cantona hasend had ~~inther~~
punishment ~~the~~ ~~~~

A further point they make is

Simmon Shouldnt have called him names
it is very nasty

However there are also strong arguments against this
point of view. its a waste~~of~~ believe that its no
good to ~~st~~ children'
time going to watch a because they will
football ~~match~~ when somethink copey.

They say that nasty happis
Cantona did nothing to provoke
the swearing.

Furthermore they claim that lesson
Cantona has ~~learnt~~ his ~~lesson~~ ✓

After looking at the different points of view and the
evidence for them I think Cantona has had
~~an ther~~ punishment.
~~enough~~
because
Eric . cantona has been ban and has been
taken two weeks wages of him he has
shall never do it again. 67 Discussion © EXEL

Figure 10.11 (a) First draft of a discussion frame (Cantona)

There is a lot of discussion about whether Cantona as had enough punishment for his behavior. The people who agree with this idea, such as David claim that : Cantona did not do anything to provoke the swearing. They also argue that Simmons got what he deserved. A further point is Simmons shouldn't have called him names. However there are also strong arguments against this point of view. Most of our class believe that Cantona should be punished more. They say that : Simmons could have been seriously hurt. Furthermore they claim that it he is a bad influence to children and people expect to be safe at a football match.

After looking at the different points of view and the evidence for them I think Cantona should be banned for life because Cantona should be used to abuse and learn to control his temper.

Figure 10.11 (b) A final draft following a writing frame

I want to explain why The Thu dorsandst uarts usually used Fiviers instead of road

There are several reasons for this. The chief reason is That the roads werebadsothe wheels. would breaeak and itwould take ages toget there

Another reason is Thierwerero bbers andthey would nick the horses and itwouldbe dangerous.

A further reason is the weather. IF it was raney and snowey the snow gos inthe warter it moltes in thewarter and they can stillgo on his ship.

So now you can see why the Tudors and Stuarts used shipeds instadof roodes.

Figure 10.12 An explanation frame (Tudor and Stuart transport)

prior knowledge/reaction frame. After a lively discussion and teacher modelling of the frame the children went on to write their own accounts. Figure 10.13 shows one boy's writing. It is extensive and coherent.

The final 'prompting' phrase on this frame encourages the child to pass a personal judgement on what they have learnt – 'the most interesting thing' – and it is tempting to talk about this process in terms of giving children ownership of the information they were working with.

With the support of frames many struggling children achieve their most successful pieces of writing to date. One example of this is a statemented child who received extra help on a regular basis. He and his support teacher were both thrilled by the writing he produced with the help of a frame (Figure 10.14). His self esteem was clearly enhanced by this experience for this was the most extended piece of writing he had ever produced.

The same kind of success has been reported to us by support teachers in mainstream schools, both primary and secondary, and in special schools.

Although I already knew that

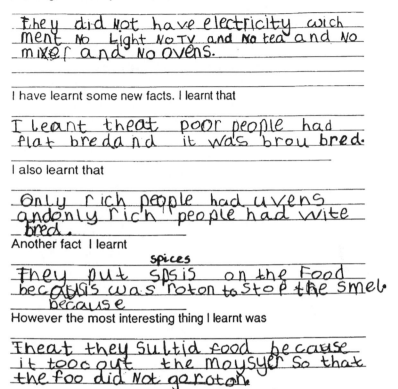

they did Not have electricity wich ment No Light NoTV and No tea and No mixer and No ovens.

I have learnt some new facts. I learnt that

I leant theat poor people had flat bredand it was brou bred.

I also learnt that

Only rich people had uvens andonly rich people had wite bred.

Another fact I learnt

spices

They put spsis on the food becpsis was roton to stop the smel. because

However the most interesting thing I learnt was

Theat they sultid food because it tooc out the moysyer so that the foo did Not garoton.

Figure 10.13 Recount frame which encourages child's opinion (the most interesting . . .)

PRODUCING YOUR OWN FRAMES

The frames we have shown are but a few of the 'general' frames that can be used in a range of writing contexts. There are many different frames (Lewis and Wray, 1995) but teachers can devise their own frames using their knowledge of generic structures and their knowledge of their class. Teachers can produce individual frames for a particular child, in a particular context with a particular writing purpose. In creating individual and/or group frames for a particular purpose the teacher can introduce a range of starter sentences and alternative connectives and guard against the same frame becoming a formulaic response.

On all occasions, however, whether using frames produced by others or teachers' own frames, it is important to be clear that the frames themselves are not a purpose for writing. The reasons for writing should arise from the work children are undertaking, the visit they have just returned from, the local issue they feel passionately about, etc. and a frame then used if the children

Before I began this topic I thought that I DID'T NO NOTN

But when I read about it I found out that teh rie verWejr teh gjk m

I also learnt that teh mnmmy Fl aDdid For thre sip ws, jk work go in bo r ss.

Furthermore I learnt that teh Gypsan poopel wisto

Finally I learnt that whsere marks.

Figure 10.14 Recount frame by a child with a statement of special needs, Year 3

need support with their writing. The frames themselves will not motivate writing and should not be used as a writing worksheet.

FROM SCAFFOLDING TO INDEPENDENCE

Children need to use frames less and less as their knowledge of writing forms increases and their confidence in their ability to write grows. At this later stage, when the child begins to show evidence of independent usage it is useful to have copies of a range of frames, mounted on card, and available as Help cards for those occasions when they may still need an occasional prompt. The frames should include those that are structured throughout such as the ones already shown and ones which are more open end such as that shown in Figure 10.15.

A box of 'Help' cards could be a part of the writing area in which children are encouraged to refer to many different aids to their writing. The writer can get a frame and have it alongside them whilst writing as a reminder that help is available if they need it. Such a support fits with the general 'procedural facilitation' strategy for children's writing suggested by Bereiter and Scardamalia (1987). It also seems to be a way into encouraging children to begin to make independent decisions about their own learning and, although some children may need scaffolding for a considerable time, other children may never need a frame or may only need to use one occasionally and for a brief time. The ultimate aim is, of course, to gradually reduce the amount of scaffolding children need and move them into independent writing.

I would like to persuade you that
There are many arguments that support my point of view. Firstly

> These words and phrases may help you in your writing.
> This shows that
> Another piece of evidence is
> A further point is
> I would also argue that
> You can see that
> This means
> Therefore

Figure 10.15 A more open form of a writing frame

CONCLUSION

As an adult, competent language user, consider how often you make use of frames for writing. Adult writing is framed in many ways – your job application form is a type of writing frame, the evaluation you are asked to complete at the end of an in-service course is usually framed in some way, the accident report form you send to your car insurance company – all these are carefully structured to help you organise and complete a comprehensive piece of writing. We find frames useful – it seems sensible to also offer such structured support to less experienced writers.

Chapter 11

Bringing it all together: Key Stage 1

THE INFANT RESEARCHER

The original title of the project from which the work described in this book grew was 'Extending Literacy in the Junior School'. It rapidly became clear, however, that the processes involved when children were researching and interacting with text are not age-specific. Levels of experience and expertise naturally vary across the age phases, as does the level of support children need, but the processed involved in interacting with information texts are essentially the same for an infant as for an adult. More support will be needed by the infant but, just as one improves as a reader by reading, one becomes more expert at 'researching' by undertaking research. Children encounter non-fiction texts (books, lists, notices, signs, etc.) from their earliest years, both in school and at home, yet most of the work on children's use of this kind of text has concentrated upon older children. For example, the only major British research so far into the use of reading as a medium for learning (Lunzer and Gardner, 1979; 1984) was undertaken with secondary and upper junior children.

The very terms used to describe research skills can seem to imply a chronological hierarchy. References to 'higher order reading skills' or 'advanced reading skills' have certainly led many teachers to feel that the teaching of study skills is best undertaken in the later stages of the primary school, when children are competent readers. This was the model written into many school language policies in the 1970s and 1980s (e.g. dictionary work in Year 3, the use of an index in Year 4, etc.). These ideas are beginning to change and more attention has been recently given to research as a feature of the curriculum experiences offered to younger children (Mallett, 1991; Neate, 1992). We would argue that children should be introduced to non-fiction texts and how to learn from them from their earliest days in school. Indeed, the new curriculum orders for English (DfE, 1995) are quite explicit in their requirements for teachers to provide children with learning experiences, both in reading and writing, that are based on non-fiction material. At Key Stage 1 we are told that part of the range of experiences children should encounter whilst reading is that they should 'be introduced to and should read information' making use of 'a range of sources of information' (p. 6). The reading 'key skills' also include the demand that children are '... taught to use reference materials for different purposes. They should be taught about the structural devices for organising information, e.g. contents, headings, captions' (p. 8). Similarly in writing, the range of writing pupils should experience at Key Stage 1 includes the criteria that they should 'be taught to write in a range of forms, incorporating some of the different characteristics of those forms' (p. 9) and this is further elaborated in the writing 'key skills' which state 'Pupils should be helped to make choices about vocabulary and to organise imaginative and factual writing in different ways' (p. 9).

In the following case studies we will examine work in two different Key Stage 1 classrooms to show how young children can be supported as they work with non-fiction texts.

A PROCESS MODEL FOR RESEARCH TASKS

Let us briefly remind ourselves of the process model discussed in Chapter 4 (Figure 4.1, p. 31).

Process stages

1 Activation of previous knowledge. (What do I already know about this subject?)
2 Establishing purposes. (What do I need to find out and what will I do with the information?)
3 Locating information. (Where and how will I get this information?)
4 Adopting an appropriate strategy. (How should I use this source of information to get what I need?)
5 Interacting with text. (What can I do to help me understand this better?)
6 Monitoring understanding. (What can I do if there are parts I do not understand?)
7 Making a record. (What should I make a note of from this information?)
8 Evaluating information. (Should I believe this information?)
9 Assisting memory. (How can I help myself remember the important parts?)
10 Communicating information. (How should I let other people know about this?)

It should be stressed again that we do not intend this model to be interpreted as a linear description of what happens when we read for information. Rather, the process is recursive with various stages being revisited and tackled in different orders dependent upon the precise purposes of each reading experience. Different tasks and different contexts will demand different starting points and different routes. For example, the task may be to write an instructional poster to help other children use the tape recorder to listen to stories in the book corner. In such a situation the first stage of this would be establishing a purpose with communicating information firmly in mind. If, however, the task were to undertake a class topic on toys the process may well start by the teacher encouraging the children to share their existing knowledge through discussion, brain storming, etc. In this latter context, decisions about how to communicate the information may not arise until later in the process.

CASE STUDY ONE – BUDDING RESEARCHERS

Let us see now see how the process can operate in infant classrooms. In our first example, Ms C's class of Year 2 city children work in a pleasant, open plan classroom. The school is built around a central courtyard. The class are responsible for the flower beds in this courtyard and some of the children attend a lunchtime gardening club run by a classroom assistant. The school has decided to spend some money planting up hanging baskets for the courtyard areas. On this occasion the research process is starting from 'establishing purpose'. The children know they are to plan a hanging basket and the following week they are to visit the garden centre to purchase their plants. In discussion with their teacher the children quickly realise that only certain plants will be suitable for a hanging basket and in order to be successful in planning their baskets they will have to undertake some research.

Structuring the research

Their teacher guides them to make the focus for their research as explicit and structured as possible. Simply to ask them to 'find out' about plants would be much too vague and vast a task. As the children are relatively inexperienced researchers she decides that a grid will help focus their research and provide a scaffold for the kind of questions they might want to ask.

Through discussion she activates their prior knowledge of gardening, flowers and hanging baskets. As they brainstorm what they already know she scribes their comments. Certain 'themes' emerge which they draw together into several headings – height, spread, colour, flowers and leaves, smell. Together they construct a grid and the children then copy this grid into their jotters (see Figure 11.1).

During the discussion and construction of the grid the teacher extended the children's technical vocabulary, substituting 'fragrance' for 'smell' and 'foliage' for 'leaves'. By introducing these words at this stage she was preparing them for the vocabulary they might encounter when they began to look in books. The books they had to use were mainly adult gardening books and their vocabulary, layout and print size made no concessions to infant

name of flower	colour	height	fragrance	spread	trailing
pansy	purple	15 cm			
(b) petunia	pink	23 cm			
Fuschia	pink purple	50 cm			✓
nasturtium	red, orange, yellow	30 cm 25 cm			
French marigold	orange yellow	30 cm			
Lobelia		30 cm		6 in	
(Bizzy) Busy Lizzie		(6) 25 cm		6-9	

Figure 11.1 Grid used to support the research

readers. Each heading of the grid acted both as a question to be answered and a 'key word' to focus the research and perhaps even to help with scanning the text for that particular word.

Before they began their research the teacher discussed with the children where they might find the information they need. The children suggested books, asking 'experts' (i.e. members of the gardening club), looking at other hanging baskets, asking their parents, watching gardening programmes on television and the teacher next modelled for them how they might select and use information books. As she did so she talked about what she was doing and why in order to make her internal monologue accessible to the children.

Now which of these books shall I use? This book's got flowers on the cover so it might be useful and the title . . . yes *Garden Flowers* that tells me it might be useful. Now what do I do? Yes, I can look in the index. Let's look up hanging baskets in the index. So I'm going to turn to the back of the book. Here it is. Index. Now. Its arranged alphabetically a . . . d . . . g . . . h . . . h . . . here it is. H. Lets look for h, a. . . .

We have already pointed out the importance of this kind of metacognitive modelling, making in making clear to children what it is an experienced reader does.

Undertaking the research

We videoed several groups of children as they undertook their research. In pairs (six children at a time) they worked around a table loaded with gardening and flower books. Their teacher checked on the group at intervals but for most of the time the children worked independently. The video recorder was left running throughout the morning and, after about 15 minutes during which they tended to whisper to each other and glance at the camera from time to time, the children seemed to become largely oblivious to its presence. Field notes and observations were also made. We were then able to view and review the video and analyse what took place. There were several striking features of the children's work that morning.

Scaffolding the task

The video evidence demonstrated how important the grid was in scaffolding and prompting the children through a very complex task of information gathering. It reminded them of what they needed to know but also allowed them space for their own interests. Several times the grid prompted children to return to the book(s) for further information. For example, Amy and Kelly had, after some searching, found a reference to Nasturtiums in the index.

Amy: Nasturtiums Nasturtiums … GOT IT … 157 … 157 … 157. (*Turning pages and checking number.*) Here. Nasturtiums. Should be here somewhere. (*Scanning page.*) There it is. Height 1 foot … 30cms. Well done. I found it.
        (*Kelly begins to write. Amy closes book.*)
Amy: I don't know the colour yet do I? [*Colour is the next column on grid.*] (*Reopens book.*) 157 … Right … What's the colour? … What's the colour? (*Reads aloud.*) Red, orange, yellow. Red, orange, yellow. We'd better get red. (*Closes book again.*)
Kelly: How do you spell …? (*Both write in colour column.*)
Amy: (*Looking at grid.*) Right. Fragrance. What's its fragrance? Has it got a fragrance or has it not? I don't think … (*Opens book and searching for page 157 again.*) Now where's it gone?

Here we see quite clearly the grid reminding Amy of what she needed to know and prompting her to continue her research. The grid acted as a scaffold for the children, helping them move from the stage of joint action with a more experienced teacher towards independent action.

The grid also encouraged the children to remodel the information they were reading to fit within the grid format. This requirement for fairly specific information makes the copying of large chunks of information less likely. The importance of text restructuring has been discussed in Chapter 7.

Using study skills: practice in context

The children used a variety of study skills during their research. They used them because they needed to use them. We observed them using index pages, contents pages, alphabetical order, skimming, scanning and extracting key information. Of course, they did not always use these successfully and they showed varying levels of expertise but they were receiving practice in using very important skills in the best possible way.

Sometimes they learnt extremely sophisticated skills. Amy and Kelly, for example, in looking up 'Busy Lizzy' found the entry: 'Busy Lizzy – see Impatiens'. Puzzled by this, they sensibly approached their teacher for an explanation. Very few teachers of six year olds would plan to introduce their pupils to the use of Latin plant names and yet occurring as it did, within the context of a real situation, these children were fascinated by their discovery. They also learnt about cross-referencing in an index. How many study skills programmes would introduce cross referencing to six year olds? Yet Amy and Kelly took it in their stride.

Most of the children were also willing to try several different techniques if their first attempt to find an answer failed. Here is Amy again, starting her hunt for Nasturtiums and trying a variety of strategies.

Amy: This one got anything? (*Picks up a book.*)
Kelly: I need to copy. (*Looks at the spelling of nasturtiums in Amy's jotter and writes.*)
Amy: Index. It should be here somewhere. Yes ... right ... what does it say? ... Nasturtiums. ... It hasn't got it there. I'll have to go to the contents. Turn to the front. Ah, here it is. (*Searches contents page.*)
Amy: It'll have to be another book. (*Scans pile of books on offer.*)
Kelly: Look in that one. (*Points to book.*)
Amy: Yeah. I'll look in this one. (*Picks up book Kelly indicated.*)
Kelly: (*Holds front cover with Amy.*) What's it say? (*Reads.*) Ornamental Kitchen Garden.
Amy: This is the one I had. (*Browsing through some pages of pictures, but actively searching.*) This tells us about ... hardy Petunias ... French Marigolds ... Nasturtiums? ... Sweet Williams ... Lizzie Busies ... Lizzie Busies. Midsummer Plants. (*Reading page heading.*) Marigolds. I've got some in my back yard.
      (*Muttered conversation between the two. Keep on 'browse searching'.*)
Amy: Where's it gone? Nasturtium.
Kelly: Have a look in another book.
      (*Amy and Kelly each pick up another book.*)
Kelly: Have a look in the index.
Amy: Index. Right.
      (*Both looking in index of their book.*)
Amy: Nasturtiums ... Nasturtiums ... GOT IT. ...

As well as the structured techniques of using the index and contents pages the children also used less structured techniques such as random searching, skimming through looking for pictures, and flicking over pages. These techniques can also achieve results, however and it is important that we do not over emphasis a rigid index/contents only approach to using information books. A flexible approach is more helpful especially as many information books are not organised terribly well. These children's relative inexperience in research meant they had no fixed ideas about what they should do to locate information. They were therefore willing to try a range of strategies rather than fixate upon one which, if it had not worked, might have left them unable to continue.

Using alternative sources of information

That these children had a flexible approach was also apparent in their willingness not only to use a variety of research strategies, but also a variety of information sources. As well as consulting the books, we observed children sharing their prior knowledge, asking 'experts' and using concrete examples. It was clear that the collaborative, social nature of the task was important in allowing the children to make use of these sources. Here are Lisa and Barry.

Teacher: (*to Lisa*) Do you know what a fuschia is?
Barry: (*Who is a member of the gardening club, interrupts and is ignored.*) Yes. We've got them in the garden.
Teacher: (*to Lisa*) Do you know what colour it is? Have a look in the index.
Barry: Yes. We've got one in the garden (*pointing*).
Teacher: (*to Lisa*) You can look up fuschia in the index or you can talk to Barry about it. He seems to know a lot about it. (*Teacher leaves.*)
Barry: (*to Lisa*) You can look over there. We've got one over there. I've seen it thousands of times.
Lisa: (*Searching for a particular page in a book having looked in the index.*) Is that it there?
            (*Shows him a picture. They both look.*)
Barry: What? In there? ... Do you want to look out of the window and I'll show you?
Lisa: (*With mock reluctance, getting up.*) Oh ...
            (*Both go to the window.*)
Barry: (*pointing*) That one there. See that one there.
            (*Lisa nods.*)

The children remained at the window for about a minute and were joined by another child who also wanted to look before being ushered back to their seats by a passing adult. On her way back to the table Lisa remarked to Barry that the fuschia in the garden were a different colour to the one in the picture, a fact she was to record in her grid, where she wrote 'purple and pink or they can be white' (see Figure 11.1).

In this brief incident we see Barry clearly determined to display his expertise and able to use his past experience and the availability of real examples to share his knowledge with his peers. Lisa learnt something about using different sources of information and she noticed that they don't always agree (they offered her different colours).This was an important lesson in becoming a critical reader.

Empowerment through information

Two of the children we observed learnt a very important lesson that morning. We often talk about empowering children. Lorraine and Charlotte learnt that knowledge can be very powerful.

The pair had begun by browsing through the gardening books, looking at pictures. From these pictures they decided that they wanted their hanging basket to contain tomatoes, strawberries and a bonsai tree. They wrote the names of these three plants into the first column of their grid and were about to start looking for further information when their teacher joined them. She pointed out that their choice was unusual and maybe that was because they were not suitable plants and perhaps they might have to change their minds. Charlotte and Lorraine were not deflected from their original choice and started to research. In the tomato section of a book they discovered a variety of dwarf trailing tomatoes. Then they turned to bonsai trees. They discovered a section on the growing and training of bonsai trees. This gave them the information that bonsai trees could be trained into shape (see Figure 11.2). They reasoned that they could train their bonsai tree to trail over their basket. They worked out that they would need wire for this task but they did fail to realise that it might take them 50 years to grow their tree! When their teacher returned they were ready to argue their case.

They had learnt that, armed with information, you can argue with powerful and important people such as your teacher. Knowledge can give you the power to argue your case – a lesson central to democracy. Their teacher was humane and responsive enough to concede the argument.

Communicating results

After they had undertaken their research all the children gathered together as a class and were able to orally share their findings before together they made a class decision as to the flowers they were going to purchase. The final communication of their research was apparent a month later, by which time their completed hanging baskets had become an attractive feature of the school courtyard. They gave the children much pleasure, pride and satisfaction as well as providing a clear example of the rewards of successful research.

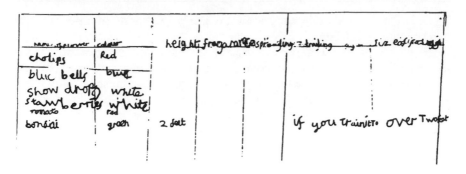

Figure 11.2 A partially completed grid

CASE STUDY 2

In this second case study we follow four groups of Key Stage 1 children as they read and wrote for information and see again how, with teacher modelling and appropriate scaffolding within a curriculum context, they

- learned to use the reading for information 'key skills' mentioned for their age group (and some of those mentioned only at Key Stage 2 such as scanning, skimming, using indexes),
- developed their factual writing,
- developed some level of self awareness of what it is you do when you are dealing with information,
- began to make independent decisions on the appropriate strategies to adopt when seeking for information.

The classes

The children involved in this case study were Year 2 mixed ability groups from a primary school built in the 1950s to serve an extensive council estate on the edge of a city. The school had been giving thought as to how it could develop the reading, writing and using of information texts by its pupils. It was planned to embed the development of 'research skills' in the on-going topic work of the classes so that the very activity of using 'real' information books would almost inevitably lead to opportunities for the teaching of 'information retrieval skills' (an important, but only a small part, of the process) at the point of need, rather than as separate exercises.

Growing and changing

For the Year 2 classes the Spring term marked the start of a new topic particularly appropriate to the changing seasons: 'growing and changing'. The school was full of bulbs and seeds being planted; growth observations being recorded; photographs of babies, children and adults being compared; children being measured and their statistics recorded; trips were being arranged to a nearby country park to see young animals, and to a local forest to see seedlings and fully grown trees; life cycles being investigated; stories read (*The Very Hungry Caterpillar, Titch*, etc.). In short, a range of rich and varied experiences were offered to the children in which opportunities for learning were plentiful.

Using big books and introducing indexes

'They should be taught about the structural devices for organising information, e.g. contents, headings, captions' (DfE, 1995, p. 8).

Reading aloud to children is an established part of Key Stage 1 classrooms. Story time is an important part of the day and teachers try to ensure that children experience of a wide range of story texts – traditional tales, stories based on contemporary experiences, fantasy, adventure and so on. We know that such 'immersion' is vital in helping children become familiar with the structures, patterns and rhythms of written texts and such 'lessons' are as important for non-fiction texts as for fiction texts. Using fiction big books is well established as an aid to inducting children into story reading and non-fiction big books can offer the same opportunities for information reading. They enable teachers to undertake teacher modelling with a group of children 'to make explicit the structure and organisation of information texts' (Monk, Davies and Karavis, 1992).

The Year 2 children were looking at life cycles and the first session began with a group sharing a big book, *The Life of a Duck* ('Magic Beans' series, 1989). The same session was repeated for groups from each of the two parallel classes so that the sessions could be compared. The teacher had brought in a duck's egg and after discussing the front cover of the book with the children (getting them to predict what they thought the book might have in it – prediction is one way of activating prior knowledge) she asked them to say what they thought the link was between the book and the egg she was holding. They already knew that ducks came from eggs so they were then asked how the egg changed into the duck. No-one was quite sure so the teacher then suggested that the information book might help them ... 'But we don't want to read it all if we only want to know about eggs. I wonder if there's any way of just finding the bits about eggs?' In each group at least two children responded that there was a list of words at the back and at the front that told you where to look. Mrs M then explicitly modelled the use of the index. When they had located an appropriate page she then used the format to discuss the structural features of the text with the children.

Mrs M: What's this writing in bigger type for I wonder? Here at the top of
            the page. 'Hatching.' It tells us what this page is about. We call it

a heading. Are there any more headings? Oh yes, look here and here (*turns to pages 8 and 9*).

Harry: The letters are bigger.

Mrs M: Yes they're in bigger, blacker letters – and on a line on their own. That's what headings are like. What does it say? 'The embryo'. I wonder what that means? It looks from the pictures as though there is a lot about eggs on this page. If we read it we might find out what an embryo is. (*Reads page aloud, inviting comments/questions as she reads.*)

The teacher and children continued to share the book in this way concentrating only on the information about eggs and with the teacher continuing to point out structural devices and continuing to talk about what she was doing and why, as well as reading out loud the relevant information they had located. After sharing the big book together in this way the children were then given the standard size version of the same book and told that they could look for information on eggs themselves. Whilst they browsed through the books, four of the children referred back and forwards to the index as their teacher had demonstrated, one turned the pages apparently looking at the headings and one child appeared to go through looking at the pictures to guide him. Ben, sitting next to him, nudged him and said 'Use the index' but Adrian preferred to continue concentrating on the pictures. The session with the second group followed a similar pattern with no major differences between the two groups although only three children in the second group spontaneously used the index. With both groups it was clear that the teacher modelling had influenced how the children then used the books when given a subsequent opportunity for individual reading/browsing.

From modelling to independent action

Having introduced the use of an index using the big book, in a later session the children were encouraged to find out the ingredients needed to make bread (they had first made an egg sandwich) using a variety of reference books selected from the library. Some of these contained an index, some did not. It was considered important that the children should be aware that not all reference books are well organised for information seeking and that other strategies might be needed. Several children commented on the lack of an index in some of the books and tended to discard the book in favour of one that had an index. The word 'bread' was written on a card for the children and they used this to scan down the index and match the word when they found it. (See Chapter 7 for a fuller description of this strategy.) The abler children quickly abandoned physically running the card down the index/page but the less confident readers continued to use this strategy appearing to find it a supportive aid. Some of the abler children seemed to quickly internalise the process and indeed seemed to find it worthy of note in itself (Figures 11.3 and 11.4).

It could be argued that such comments provide evidence of metacognitive awareness, on the part of these individuals, as to the process they were using.

Text restructuring

Having undertaken some research involving using reference books, the teacher then wanted the children to make some record of what they had learnt. After completing the 'big book' reading on ducks/eggs and drawing diagrams of the egg (which had been cracked open) it was suggested to the children that they could write about what they had learnt. Kim (group 2) replied 'Can I write what it says here' and Christopher said 'I want to copy this' pointing to an apparently random piece of text in the book. In order to encourage original responses the teacher therefore helped this group compose an opening sentence which she scribed: 'We already knew that ducks laid eggs' before orally adding 'And now we know ...?'. The effect of teachers' oral promptings is well understood, and much used, by all classroom teachers and Bereiter and Scardamalia (1987) have shown how such oral promptings

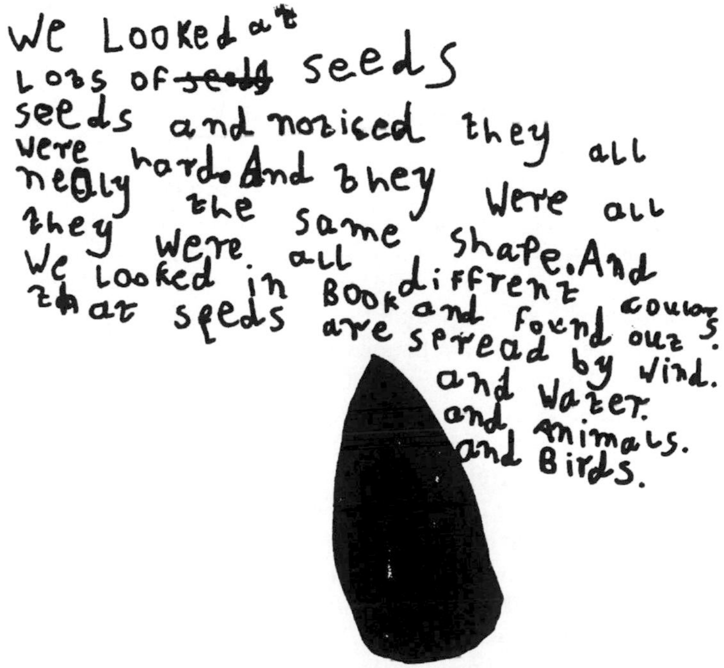

Figure 11.3 Comments on the research process included in the writing: Example 1

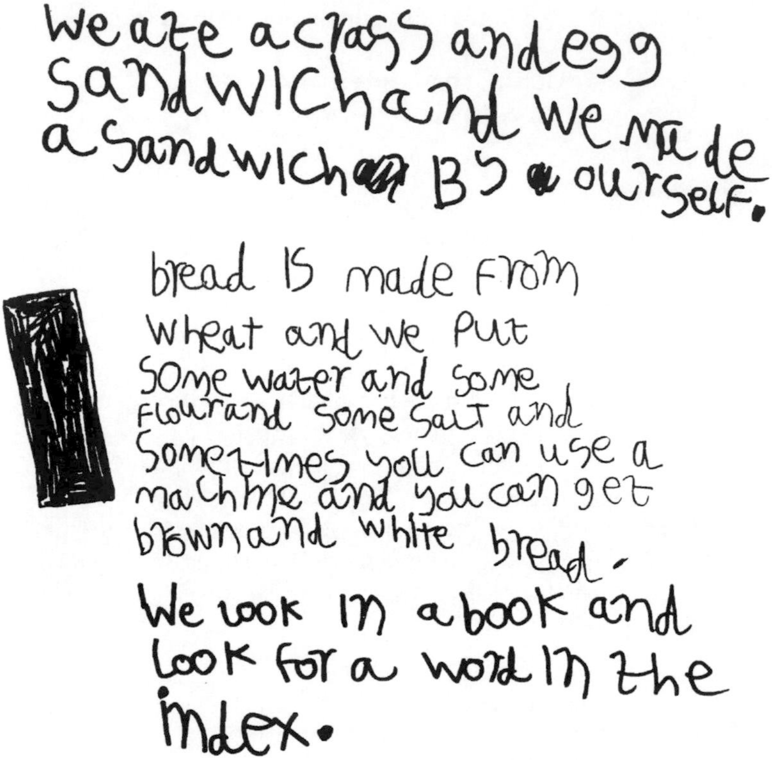

We ate a class and egg
Sandwich and we made
a sandwich B5 ourself.

bread is made from
wheat and we put
some water and some
flour and some salt and
sometimes you can use a
machine and you can get
brown and white bread.
We look in a book and
look for a word in the
index.

Figure 11.4 Comments on the research process included in the writing: Example 2

scaffold and extend children's writing (see Chapter 10). The children responded orally and then wrote.

In another strategy to move these children away from copying the teacher puzzled aloud. 'We've learnt a lot about how eggs turn into ducks I wonder how we could show that information for those in the class who don't read as well as you do? They might not be able to read your work.' The teacher was encouraging the children to come up with their own ideas on how to show the information in the text in some other way than writing. They came up with the idea of using pictures and joining them with arrows. This activity was extended for the more able children in the group by getting then to label their flow diagram and add time information (Figure 11.5).

The other Year 2 group were not asked to write about what they had learnt but taken straight into text remodelling 'How can we show what we learnt in another way – something different from the book?' Harry suggested we could number it 1, 2, 3 and say what happens. He was trying to suggest a sequential account and the group went on to try this (Figure 11.6).

Eventually children start to internalise such strategies and develop their

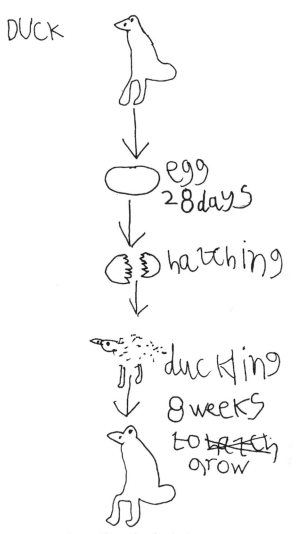

Figure 11.5 Text restructuring – life cycle of a duck

own ways of 'showing that information in another way'. Not only does it show them moving into making independent decisions about their own learning but the accuracy of their remodelling also demonstrates their level of understanding of a text. Some children needed considerable support and suggestions on ways of possible remodelling before it became an independent strategy but other children 'got the point' very quickly. The week following her work on eggs, when she had been helped to devise a flow diagram, Kim had planted cress seeds. In order to take some seeds home to plant she was making a seed packet. Modelling her packet on actual seed packets the group

Figure 11.6 Text restructuring – sequential chart

had examined, she wrote on the back and did a label and illustration on the front. She then asked 'Can I draw one of those things? Those things that tell you about things?' Intrigued, but a little puzzled, her teacher assented and Kim proceeded to draw a flow diagram of the growth of seeds (Figure 11.7). Pointing to it she was able to explain that the man planted the seeds and the water came and the flowers grew. Then more rain and more sun and the flowers grew some more.

Over the next few weeks other children also began to offer their own independent text remodelling work, as an alternative to writing, such as Ben's flow diagram on making a cress sandwich (Figure 11.8).

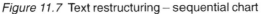

Figure 11.7 Text restructuring – sequential chart

FINAL POINT

These case studies show that young children, given the right kind of support, are certainly capable of engaging with non-fiction texts in order to learn. This definitely suggests to us that ideas about 'advanced' and 'higher order' skills are a long way from what is really needed to capitalise on their potential in this area.

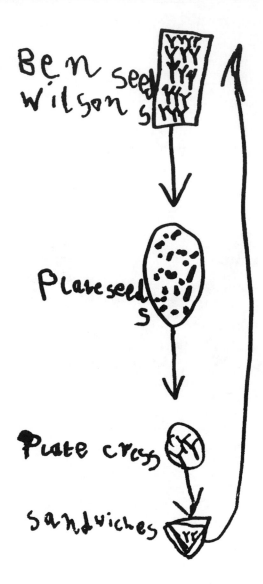

Figure 11.8 Text restructuring – flow diagram to show how to make a cress sandwich

Chapter 12

Bringing it all together: Key Stage 2

Throughout the book we have illustrated our argument with examples of children's work. In this final chapter we will carry on this process and focus on two further, important issues. These are, first, how can a knowledge of the research process we have described and illustrated be used to support less able children in undertaking research tasks? And second, how can the process be used to support a term's work in a Key Stage 2 classroom? Our application of the process in both these contexts will also allow us to make some important points by way of summarising our work.

THE PROCESS IN USE WITH CHILDREN WITH SPECIAL NEEDS

From our work with teachers we are convinced that the process of learning with non-fiction texts remains exactly the same for children with special needs as for any other children. As we have argued earlier, we reject the concept of higher-order, or advanced reading skills as a way of describing such learning with text. We suggest, however, that for children with reading and/or learning problems an even greater emphasis needs to be placed on particular features of the teaching approaches we have been describing. These features are:

- the group discussion of concepts. Children working alongside others more knowledgeable than themselves can be supported in their learning by the shared knowledge which the group can generate. We discussed the concepts of shared and borrowed consciousness in Chapter 3;
- teacher modelling;
- explicit discussion of processes;
- the breaking down of processes into small steps;
- the use of supportive strategies;
- the opportunity to practise skills within a context.

CHILDREN WITH LITERACY DIFFICULTIES USING INFORMATION TEXTS – A CASE STUDY

The following scene might have occurred in many classrooms. The learning support teacher arrives to find that Zoe, along with the rest of the class, has been asked to 'find out about whales and dolphins'. Zoe has been working hard for sometime and this is what she had written.

She cannot read this work back to her support teacher and has only the vaguest understanding of what she has written. She has clearly copied, word for word, from a book. Why is this? Our earlier research (Wray and Lewis, 1992) has suggested that most children are aware that they should not copy directly from books. Many can give sound educational reasons for this (e.g. 'you learn more if you put it in your own words'), and yet they continue to do so. There appear to be several reasons for this but an important one appears to be the nature of the task the child has been given to do and the type of text with which they are asked to engage when reading for information.

The purpose of 'finding out' may not be clear to the child and how to begin to 'find out' may seem difficult and daunting. Having located a book the child might still find the text difficult to deal with. Children in primary classrooms tend to lack experience of the different genres of non-fiction and their organisational structures (Littlefair, 1991; Winograd and Bridge, 1986). They

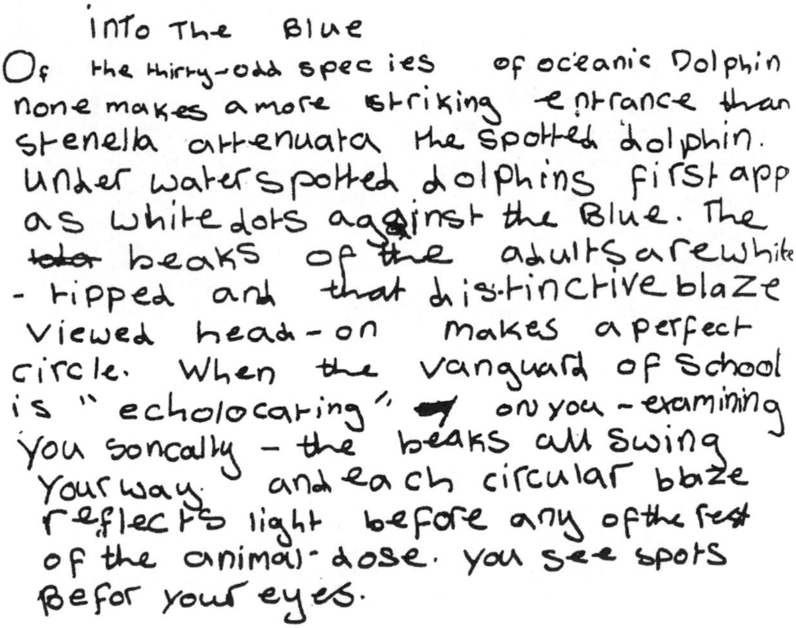
Into The Blue
Of the thirty-odd species of oceanic Dolphin none makes a more striking entrance than stenella attenuata the spotted dolphin. under waterspotted dolphins first app as white dots aggainst the Blue. The ~~tota~~ beaks of ~~the~~ adults are white - tipped and ~~that~~ distinctive blaze viewed head-on makes a perfect circle. When the vanguard of school is "echolocating" on you - examining you soncally - the beaks all swing your way. and each circular blaze reflects light before any of the rest of the animal dose. you see spots Befor your eyes.

Figure 12.1 Zoe's first attempt at writing about whales

find the linguistic features (vocabulary, connectives, cohesion, register) more difficult to comprehend than those of the more familiar narrative texts (Chapman, 1983; Halliday and Hasan, 1976; Littlefair, 1991) and this textual inexperience affects their writing of non-fiction as well as their reading (see Chapter 10). In the case of Zoe, the problem was further compounded by the child's poor literacy skills (relative to her age). Her diligent copying was the only strategy she had for coping with the demands of the task.

A different approach

Zoe's support teacher has been working with the EXEL project and she decided to introduce Zoe to a different way of approaching her task. At the end of their hour together Zoe had produced a different piece of writing about dolphins and whales (see Figure 12.2).

The first step had been to close Zoe's library book and introduce her to a KWL grid (see Chapters 4 and 5). The KWL grid gives children a logical

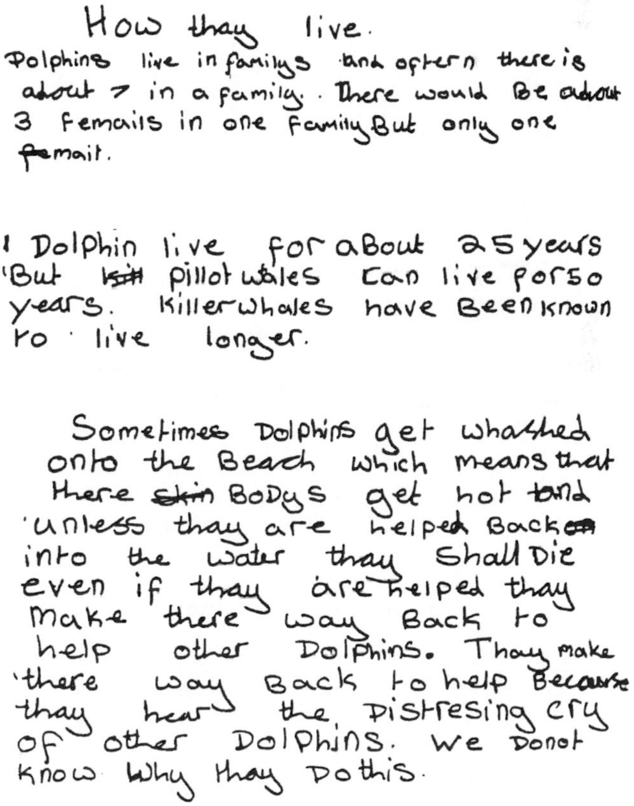

How thay live.
Polphins live in familys and oftern there is about 7 in a family. There would Be about 3 femails in one FamilyBut only one femait.

I Dolphin live for aBout 25 years 'But pillot wales Can live porso years. KillerWhales have Been known ro live longer.

Sometimes Dolphins get whashed onto the Beach which means that there Bodys get hot and 'unless thay are helped Back into the water thay Shall Die even if thay are helped thay make there way Back to help other Dolphins. Thay make 'there way Back to help Because thay hear the Distresing cry of other Dolphins. we Donot know Why thay Do this.

Figure 12.2 Zoe's second attempt

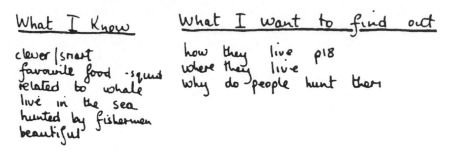

Figure 12.3 Zoe's teacher scribes a KWL

structure for tackling research tasks in many areas of the curriculum and it is this combination of a simple but logical support scaffolding that seems to be so useful to children with learning difficulties. Zoe's support teacher introduced her to the strategy by drawing a KWL as three columns in Zoe's jotter. She then asked Zoe what she already knew about whales/dolphins and acted as a scribe to record Zoe's responses. What Zoe knew can be seen in the K column of Figure 12.3. In the introductory stages of teaching the strategy, as for most new strategies and skills, teacher modelling is very important. Only when the child is thoroughly familiar with the strategy should they be encouraged to attempt it independently.

Not only does the activation of prior knowledge have a vital role to play in helping Zoe comprehend the texts she was to read, but it also gave her an active role in the topic right from the beginning. By asking her what she knew, her self esteem and sense of 'ownership' of knowledge was enhanced instead of her being faced instantly with the (for her) negative experience of tackling a text without knowing quite how she was to make sense of it. This activity prior to reading is not text avoidance but text preparation. The discussion between Zoe and her teacher was crucial at this stage and the activation of prior knowledge should always be an active social process. Sometimes we do not actually know what we know until it is triggered for us by discussion. This discussion could, of course, also take place in partnership with another child or in groups with other children rather than with a teacher.

Establishing purposes (What do I want to know?)

The next stage helped focus the subsequent research. The discussion and recording of what she already knew was enough to generate further questions for Zoe – questions which she would be interested in researching. These were again scribed by the teacher (see the L column of Figure 12.3). It is tempting here to talk about giving the child some ownership of the work she is to undertake. On this occasion Zoe and her teacher decided to concentrate on just one question (they had only an hour together) and she was encouraged to brainstorm around her 'How do they live?' question. Again her teacher scribed and the resultant concept map can be seen in Figure 12.4.

The sub-questions generated by this procedure were numbered to keep the process clear and manageable and at this point Zoe was ready to return to her library books to try to find the answers to her questions. Now Zoe also had key words which she could use to search the index/contents, etc. Her teacher wrote the word on a piece of card for her so that she could run it down the index/page and match the word. This gave her practice in scanning. We can see from the writing she had completed by the end of the session (Figure 12.2) that she was working her way logically through the questions (she had completed 1 and 2) and not only had she learnt something about dolphins but she had also had a powerful lesson on how to begin research.

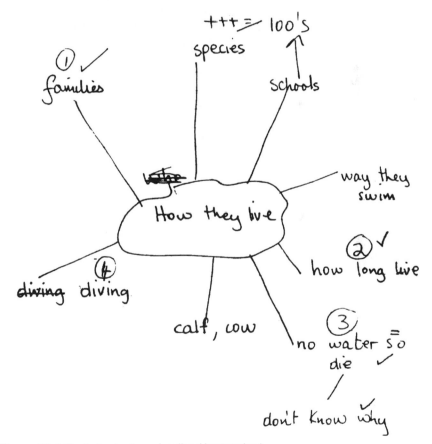

Figure 12.4 Zoe's brainstorm (scribed by teacher)

FROM EXTERNAL TO INTERNAL SCAFFOLD

Perhaps the usefulness of this process of making research accessible to less able children can be judged by whether the children, having been introduced to it by their support teacher, choose to use it spontaneously when their support teacher is not with them. Baker and Brown (1984) have suggested that students do not gain any long term benefits from study strategies until they start to incorporate these strategies spontaneously for themselves, signalling that they understand how and why they work.

An example of this happening is the case of James. He was introduced to the two process stages and the use of KWL by his support teacher when working on the topic of Ancient Greece. Notice how his listing of what he knows (Figure 12.5) also enables his teacher to see his misconceptions (medals were not given at the Olympic Games in Ancient Greece) as well as things he does know. His KWL grid, scribed by his teacher, then acted as the basis for his subsequent writing on the topic (see Figure 12.6) which was a very extensive piece of work for James.

James had obviously found the strategy useful because the following week his support teacher returned to find that he had spontaneously used it again in his next piece of topic work. This time the class was finding out about the home life of Athenians. James had drawn three columns in his jotter and although he hadn't labelled them – why give yourself extra writing if writing is a problem? – he had used the middle column to set himself four questions and was ticking these off as he gathered the information to answer them (see Figure 12.7). His subsequent writing indicates how the questions may also have suggested the structure of the finished piece.

Activating prior knowledge and establishing purposes are obviously only two stages of the process we have been describing in this book but we can see clearly how breaking a complex process down into manageable stages and providing supportive strategies that children can apply themselves can provide a helpful and rewarding way into research tasks for children with learning difficulties.

CLASS STUDY: THE PROCESS AT WORK IN KEY STAGE 2 CLASSROOM

Ms M's class of Year 4 children were studying 'change' as their term's topic. As part of the topic their teacher wished to look at how the town in which the children lived had changed over time. She also wanted the children to use contemporary documents as well as more usual information sources such as books for their research.

Like most teachers, Ms M was concerned that her pupils should begin to develop good research habits but she wanted them to learn what are often called 'study skills' within the context of real information handling tasks, rather than as isolated skills lessons. There was, of course, the usual wide range of ability and differing levels of literacy competence within the class and although she was convinced that all children should undertake what HMI describe as 'the threefold process of formulating appropriate questions, selecting and reading texts to find information and writing it up in their own words' (DES, 1989), she was worried that some of the children might find this a difficult task. Ms M had been working with the EXEL project and was interested to see how the ideas and strategies suggested by the project might

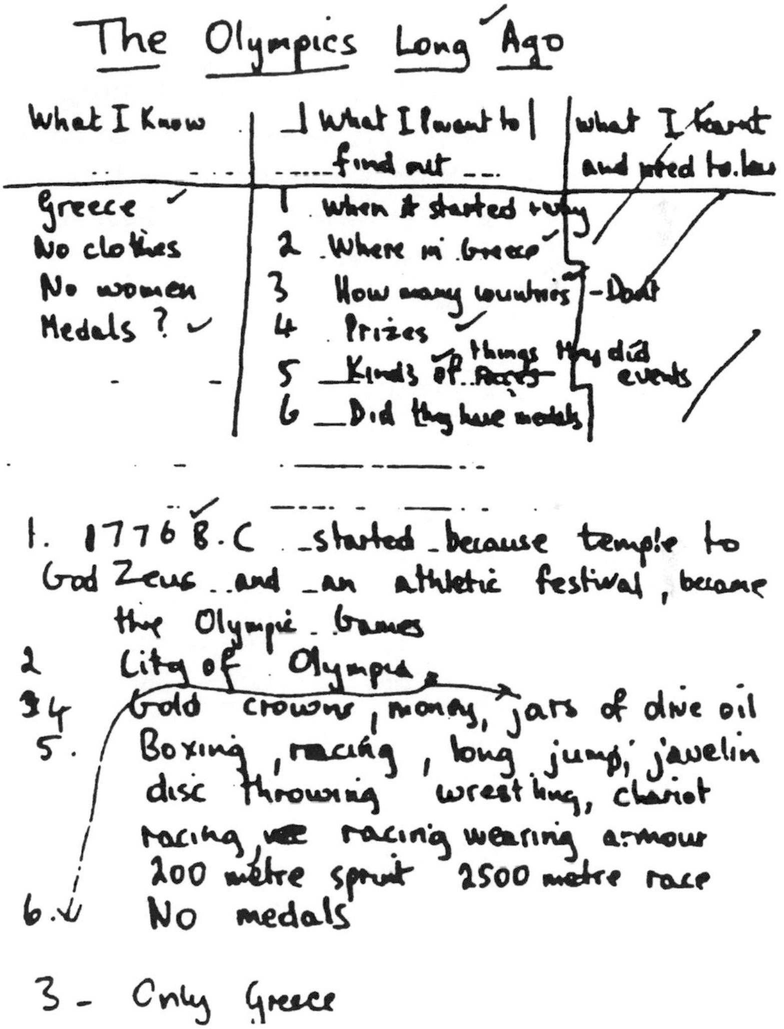

The Olympics Long Ago

What I Know	What I want to find out	What I learnt and need to know
Greece ✓	1. when it started why	
No clothes	2. Where in Greece	
No women	3. How many countries — Dont	
Medals ? ✓	4. Prizes ✓	
	5. Kinds of races — things they did events	
	6. Did they have medals	

1. 1776 B.C started because temple to God Zeus and an athletic festival, became the Olympic Games

2. City of Olympia

3 4. Gold crowns, money, jars of olive oil

5. Boxing, racing, long jump, javelin disc throwing wrestling, chariot racing racing wearing armour 200 metre sprint 2500 metre race

6. ✓ No medals

3 - Only Greece

Figure 12.5 James's KWL (scribed by teacher)

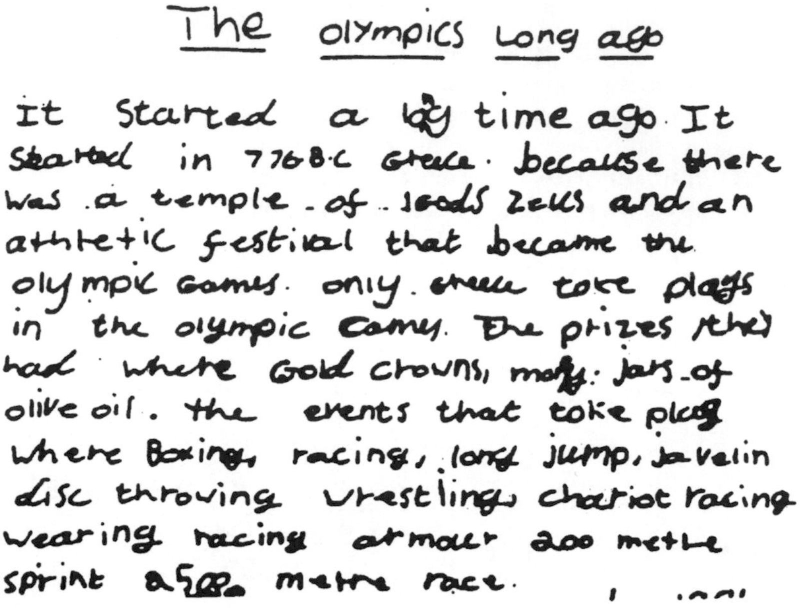

The olympics long ago

It Started a big time ago. It
Started in 776 B.C Greece. because there
was a temple of Ieods Zeus and an
athletic festival that became the
olympic Games. only Greece toke plaes
in the olympic Camy. The prizes (the)
had where Gold crowns, may. Jars of
olive oil. the events that toke pleag
where Boxing, racing, long jump, javelin
disc throving vrestling chariot racing
wearing racing armour 200 mette
sprint a 500 metre race.

Figure 12.6 James's writing

work in her classroom to help develop her pupils' interactions with non-fiction texts.

Planning the topic

Before the topic began Ms M had gathered, in the classroom, a collection of books linked to the topic together with photographs, maps, local shop advertisements from various eras, a variety of historical sources and some artefacts. She intended to take the class on a walk along the High Street and to the parish church. Although she had planned the main historical events she wished to cover (the Great Fire of Crediton, the Civil War, changes in the High Street and what that showed about changes in shopping habits, etc.) Ms M wanted the children themselves to be involved in the more detailed question setting.

The first session began with the teacher wanting to activate the children's prior knowledge about the Great Fire of Crediton. Sometimes prior knowledge is readily accessible (for example, most child will come up with something about space or families or other such topics) and the children can go straight into brainstorming, concept mapping, KWL grids, etc. However, when Ms M asked the class what they knew about the Great Fire of Crediton their answers were ones all teachers will recognise: 'Nothing . . . I don't know anything. . . . Never heard of it.' Such responses are discussed in Chapter 5.

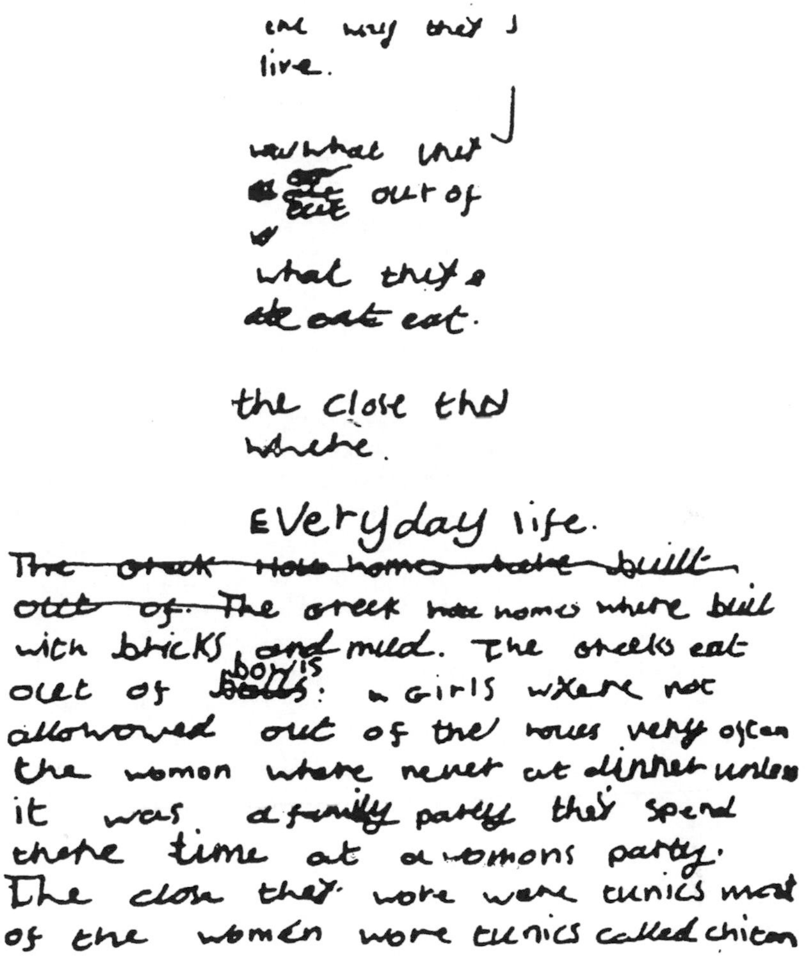

the way they J
live.

what that J
~~out~~ out of

what they
~~ate out~~ eat.

the close they
where.

Everyday life.
~~The greek Have homes where built~~
~~out of.~~ The greek had homes where built
with bricks, and mud. The greeks eat
out of ~~bows~~ bowls: Girls where not
allowowed out of the house very often
the woman where never at dinner unless
it was a family party they spend
there time at a womons party.
The clos they wore were tunics most
of the women wore tunics called chiton

Figure 12.7 James's independent KWL and subsequent writing

In this case the teacher probed their knowledge with a series of questions:

> What can you work out from the fact that it was called the Great Fire of Crediton? What does the word 'great' tell you?'

Here she was asking the children to deduce. Deduction is based on existing knowledge.

It was big. . . . It was in Crediton.
What happens when you get a big fire?
People try to put it out. . . . There is damage. . . . Buildings get destroyed. . . .
Sometimes people get killed.

These replies show the children drawing on their existing, generic knowledge of fires.

Once this discussion started several children then remembered that they had heard of the Great Fire of Crediton before. This episode clearly illustrates the importance of the social nature of activating prior knowledge – often our memories need jogging and talking with others is an important such trigger.

The teacher scribed the responses on a flip chart and when the children actually began to recall what they knew about the Great Fire of Crediton one child contributed the information that it started in a baker's shop. This was incorrect (the child was probably confusing it with the Great Fire of London). Here we can see another important aspect of activating prior knowledge. Not only did the teacher have access to what the children knew, and the gaps in their knowledge, but, importantly, she also had access to their misconceptions. She did not correct this misconception by immediately providing the correct information but scribed the comment whilst mentally noting that if no-one else suggested that one of their research questions should concern where and how the fire started, she would make sure it was included. Often misconceptions that are merely corrected by the teacher will fail to have much impact upon the children who will simply hold on to them. Children are far more likely to change their minds if they play an active part in correcting their mistakes. A common example of this is a child's spelling error corrected by the teacher but still repeated in subsequent rewritings.

Once she had listed the children's responses, the teacher read them back to the children, thus reviewing what they knew, and she then asked them if there was anything they wanted to know about the fire (establishing purposes). Questions came quickly: When was it? How did it start? Were people killed?

Again the teacher scribed the questions and at this point was able to put a question mark after the, 'It started in a baker's shop' statement. Turning statements, whether correct or incorrect, into questions is a useful question-setting strategy.

Ms M then asked the children how and where they thought they might find the answers to their questions (locating information) and they came up with a range of suggestions: books, newspapers, interviews with people who were there, photographs and television reports. This was a good list for a contemporary event but it was then pointed out to the children that as this had happened a long time ago not all these sources might apply. They went through the list, reassessing the sources, and as it was a local event the children also discussed why they might find it unproductive to look in the general history books available in the classroom.

Ms M then produced ten historical sources including eyewitness accounts, newspaper reports, insurance company accounts, disaster fund appeals, etc. and explained what each was but did not read them to the children. They were then told that they were each going to decide which question/s they wanted to research and that their final piece of work would be displayed, along with the sources, on the wall in the corridor (establishing purposes, communicating information). They were each given a QUADS sheet to record their work (see Figure 12.8) and in pairs or small groups were given a set of sources (photocopied) to share.

Having decided on, and written down, their questions the children of Class M turned to the sources. A certain amount of initial browsing went on and children shared comments and puzzlement with their partner (the shape of the *s* for example looked more like an *f* to their modern eyes). It was not possible to use contents or index pages with these document sources but the children were encouraged not to try to read the whole thing but to skim over the materials looking for key words or phrases (e.g. fire, started, died) contained in their questions. Skimming was more sensible than close reading in this initial hunt for answers (adopting an appropriate strategy). Having key words to focus their searching was especially important as the language was difficult for many of the children. Again the collaborative nature of the task was important for when the children found a section they thought might be useful they were encouraged to read it aloud with each other and to work together to try to understand what it was saying (interacting with the text/monitoring understanding). The children were actively engaged in monitoring their own understanding rather than turning instantly to the teacher to have the text read to them, although of course this remained a final option.

Several of the children discovered that different sources gave different

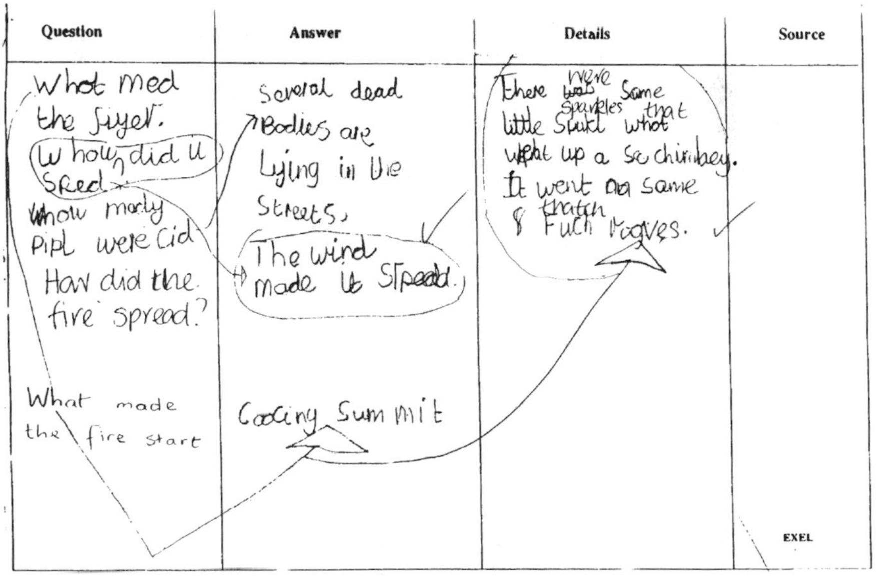

Question	Answer	Details	Source
What med the fiyer. (W holi, did u speed? whow marly pipl were cid How did the. fire spread?	Several dead bodies are Lying in the streets, The wind made it speed.	There were some little Stukl what what up a se chiribey. It went na same q futch moqves.	
What made the fire start	Cocing Sum mit		EXEL

Figure 12.8 QUADS grid on the great fire of Crediton

information, for example about how many people died and how many buildings were destroyed and this both demonstrated to them the importance of recording the source but also the importance of questioning the credibility of the sources (evaluating information). They were encouraged to try to think for themselves why a newspaper account from the next day might say twenty houses were destroyed whilst an insurance company account written a week later gave a different figure and to decide which they thought was the more accurate figure.

The children then shared their questions and answers in a session on the carpet in order for them to get a complete picture of the event and to review and revisit their research. At this point a class flow chart or grid could have been produced to review and revisit the information but there was not time to do this on this occasion. Finally, as planned, the children produced a final version of their work to go on display (communicating information).

One small group of about four children with very poor reading ability did not undertake the research from original documents but had a simple account of the events prepared by their teacher. They had to interact with this text by sequencing it. They had, however, joined in the rest of the session along with the other members of the class. The rest of the class had been paired so that more and less able readers were working together.

A DIFFERENT TASK – A DIFFERENT ROUTE

On the occasion described above the children had gone through each of the stages of the process but different information tasks will determine different routes through the process stages and any one event may not necessarily use all the stages. Let us follow two further afternoons' work to see how the model worked in different contexts. A week later the children in this class had moved on to looking at the Civil War and how it had affected the town and its people. They had been on a walk along the High Street noting pre- and post-fire buildings (reviewing and revisiting) and had visited the Parish Church which contains a leather boot reputed to have belonged to Oliver Cromwell. Back at school they discussed the boot and its owner.

On this occasion the children moved straight into question setting. Their curiosity was already aroused by the artefact they had seen. The plaque alongside the boot had given them some information and they had also been given some brief 'on the spot' information and this had generated further questions.

The children wanted to know more about Cromwell, the clothes he wore, and also about the clothes of another group of people called the Cavaliers. However, it became clear that there was a danger that nobody was actually going to raise a key question their teacher felt the children should address: i.e. what was the Civil War about and how did it affect the country? On this occasion the teacher decided she needed to play a more active role in the question setting. She recognised that it is part of our professional role sometimes to guide and direct as well as enable children to set their own questions. These are not mutually exclusive processes – either the teacher *or* the children setting the questions – but there is a role for both. She did not, however, set the question herself but she led the children to ask the questions she wanted them to include. She divided the class into Roundheads (the term had come up in the discussion) and Cavaliers, appointed a leader for each army and got the leader to line up their army and march them around the classroom. A lively five minutes followed with children stamping around and orders being called before the two armies drew up facing each other. At this point the teacher told them that the two armies were getting ready to fight each other and had they any feelings or questions about this. Many questions arose including the question of why they were fighting – just as the teacher had planned that it should. These new questions were added to the existing questions and the children then began to research the answers. On this occasion they were working in groups with information books on their tables. Again they used QUAD sheets to record their findings. A computer program on the Civil War was also available for them to use. After some time during which children used indexes, contents, picture as sources of information, browsing, and asking each other as strategies to answer their questions the teacher drew their attention to a comparison grid on the board and the children pooled their information to complete what they could of the grid. This sharing of information not only enabled children to review and revisit their work but ensured that the children got a fuller picture of the events than they might have acquired from their individual research.

For the final communication of their personal research the children had a drawing of either a Roundhead or a Cavalier and were asked to present their information in the form of a direct question to the figure with the answer coming as a speech bubble from the mouth of the drawing. By asking the children to transform their information into direct speech the teacher was lessening the opportunities for them to copy undigested chunks of text. The technique of asking children to operate a form of 'genre exchange' is a very successful strategy for helping them restructure information and make it their own (see Chapter 7).

A FURTHER SESSION

When we returned to Class M a few weeks later the children were looking at the shops in the High Street nowadays and seeing how they might have changed from 100 years ago and 50 years ago. Their teacher wanted them to become aware of how changes in shops reflect changes in society (e.g. a video shop would not have existed 50 or 100 years ago). From their previous walk along the High Street they had a photographic record of the shops (plus, of course, their existing knowledge of a familiar street). They also had certain

Type of shop	What does it sell?	Does it exist now?	Did it exist 50 years ago?	Did it exist 100 years ago?

Figure 12.9 Grid to structure children's research

contemporary sources from about 100 years ago in the form of shop advertisements, a local trade calendar, etc. along with the current Yellow Pages and a selection of books on shops and shopping.

The teacher had prepared four large grids on sugar paper (see Figure 12.9). Each of the cells of a grid act as a question to be answered and give the children a specific focus to their research rather than the more general 'Find out about shops in the High Street' (establishing purpose).

On this occasion the teacher had prepared the grids but the children can often be involved in the creation of grids and this is another way of getting them to set their own questions and consider which are appropriate questions. The grid also provides the children with a logical structure for recording their information.

Groups of children used their prior knowledge to fill in types of shops, e.g. butchers, supermarkets, etc., and the teacher added unfamiliar types to each grid, e.g. haberdashers, chandlers, etc. The teacher ensured that her additions were different for each group. In order to fill in the next column the children had to use a variety of strategies. They used dictionaries to discover what some of the unfamiliar shop types were and then used a combination of prior knowledge, books and searching advertisements to discover what each type of shop sold. Using each source effectively involved them adopting an appropriate strategy – from alphabetical searching (dictionaries), skimming visual sources (advertisements, trade calendars), to using titles, contents and indexes (books). The teacher modelled for various children how they might use the sources as she moved around the groups and articulated her thoughts as she did so.

> You're wondering what a milliner is, are you ? Well, how could we find out about words we don't know? Yes, a dictionary might help. Now, M ... somewhere near the middle as it's in the middle of the alphabet (*flicking quickly through pages*) ... L ... nearly there (*slowing down and turning a page at a time*) L ... M ... Here we are. What letter's next? i, I want m, i. M, a ... M, a ... Ah ... M, i.

This strategy of making explicit for children the thought processes a competent language user goes through (metacognitive modelling) helps make explicit for them a process that is usually invisible. This is an important aid in helping children adopt an appropriate strategy – and one that teachers and adults have used instinctively for many years.

Two further groups of children were engaged on a different activity whose aim was to lead them to a discussion of changing shopping habits over the last hundred years. In pairs, they had itemised supermarket bills stuck on a large piece of paper. They used different colour pens to underline items they would have had to get from separate shops if the supermarket had not been there. So, for example, in red they highlighted anything they would have bought from a butcher, in blue anything from a greengrocer's and so on. This use of text-marking enabled them to organise very long lists in a useful way and they were being introduced to a new information retrieval skill – the use of text marking – in a meaningful context. Marking in different colours enabled them to quickly relocate information they had highlighted and link together items that were some distance apart on the bills.

Some of this 'sorting' they could undertake from their existing knowledge but eventually they were left with various items they could not place – tights, needles, batteries, matches, etc. They had to search the old shop advertisements, or use the index of books about shopping to see which shop would have sold that item and to discover the name of that type of shop. (Incidentally, this activity showed that the word 'grocer' appears to have totally dropped from young children's vocabulary. 'Grocer' was as unusual to them as 'haberdasher' or 'draper'. Children today are used to groceries being bought in supermarkets.)

All the children in the class knew they would be sharing their work with each other at the end of the session and that they would have to explain their findings to the rest of the class (establishing purpose/communicating information).

The sessions described above may not appear to be radically different to the kind of teaching that goes on in many of our good, primary classrooms but what was evident was that the teacher's awareness of the processes involved in interacting with text enabled her to plan into her topic specific activities for the children to experience in context. For example, the children had to adopt a variety of reading strategies in order to complete real tasks not merely to practice a skill. She was concerned not primarily with the content of the sessions (although, of course, that had some importance) but more importantly with the processes the children were undertaking to enable them to become more effective users of information. The awareness of the process had been instrumental in how this teacher planned and structured the sessions and a knowledge of the theory had informed and illuminated her practice.

CONCLUSION

This work, taken together with the case studies we have explored at Key Stages 1 and 2 shows clearly that children of all ages and abilities can become successful users of information text. We have also undertaken work with Key Stage 3 pupils using the same process model and have had equally successful results.

From the work of the EXEL project described and illustrated at length in this book, we have been left with some strong, over-riding impressions. These include the following:

- Children of all ages can be successfully introduced to effective ways of learning with texts. We have found few age or ability barriers to this kind of work and, indeed, systematically introducing children to the process we refer to as 'researching' can transform their approaches to reading and writing generally.
- The importance of the teacher as a model cannot be over-emphasised. Teacher modelling of complex cognitive activities has emerged from our research as a teaching strategy of major importance. Indeed, our work has led us to seriously question views of the teacher's role in primary classrooms which focus almost entirely upon the creation of stimulating learning environments. Of course, good teachers do this, but they also *teach* and we have found the model of teaching discussed in Chapter 3 a powerful guide to the ways teachers might profitably intervene in children's learning. This model involves four phases:
  1 *Demonstration* teacher modelling of activities, preferably accompanied by 'thinking aloud', that is, making explicit what are usually invisible thought processes.
  2 *Collaborative activity* children engage in the activities alongside the teacher and/or their peers and sufficient support is given to ensure that they do not fail at an activity but are still practising an authentic version of it.
  3 *Supported activity* some form of scaffolding is provided to support children in the activity without the teacher needing to be there all the time. Many of the strategies we have described in this book are of this type: KWL and QUADS grids, writing frames, for example.
  4 *Independent activity* children are able gradually to move towards being able to engage in activities without support, although support should remain available for some time in case it is needed.
- Context is crucial. We strongly believe, and our work has confirmed this to us, that children learn best when they learn in meaningful contexts, through authentic activities. All the most successful teaching we have witnessed (and carried out) during the EXEL project has occurred when children were excited by what they were doing and could see clearly where it was leading.

- Successful learning needs time. If we want children to do more with information than simply copy it out from a book, we need to give them time to work with it, to restructure it for different purposes, to consider and evaluate it. These processes cannot be rushed and curriculum plans which rush children through bodies of information are almost always ineffective in terms of long term learning.
- Finally: the extension of literacy in the way we have been using that concept in this book involves much, much more than 'information-retrieval skills'. If that were all there were to it, we would certainly not have had the extremely enthusiastic response we have had to our work from teachers across the country. We think that these teachers recognised what we ourselves have only recently realised fully – that, in thinking seriously about learning from, with and through texts, we are actually considering virtually all learning in school. Texts do not simply come inside books: the concept can easily be extended to include most sources of children's learning, from TV, video and computer texts to the texts which are created when people talk together. Post-modernist thinkers tell us that life is a text, in which case our concept of interacting with texts is a metaphor for all learning.

References

Alessi, S., Anderson, T. and Goetz, E. (1979) 'An investigation of lookbacks during studying', *Discourse Processes*, 2, pp. 197–212.

Anderson, T. (1980) 'Study strategies and adjunct aids', in R. Spiro, B. Bruce and W. Brewer (eds) *Theoretical Issues in Reading Comprehension*, Hillsdale, New Jersey: Lawrence Erlbaum.

Baker, C. and Freebody, P. (1989) *Children's First School Books*, Oxford: Blackwell.

Baker, L. and Brown, A. (1984) 'Metacognitive skills and reading', in D. Pearson (ed.) *Handbook of Reading Research*, New York: Longman.

Bereiter, C. and Scardamalia, M. (1987) *The Psychology of Written Composition*, Hillsdale, New Jersey: Lawrence Erlbaum.

Brown, A. (1979) 'Theory of memory and the problems of development: activity, growth and knowledge', in L. Cermak and F. Craik (eds) *Levels of Processing in Human Memory*, Hillsdale, New Jersey: Lawrence Erlbaum.

Brown, A. (1980) 'Metacognitive development and reading' in R. Spiro, B. Bruce and W. Brewer (eds) *Theoretical Issues in Reading Comprehension*, Hillsdale, New Jersey: Erlbaum.

Cairney, T. (1990) *Teaching Reading Comprehension*, Milton Keynes: Open University Press.

Chapman, J. (1983) *Reading Development and Cohesion*, Milton Keynes: Open University Press.

Child, D. (1973) *Psychology and the Teacher*, London: Holt, Rinehart & Winston.

Christie, F. (1985) *Language Education*, Oxford: Oxford University Press.

Cox, C. and Marshall, J. (1994) 'Strategies for enabling young readers to interact with non-fiction texts', in M. Lewis and D. Wray (eds) *Aspects of Extending Literacy*, papers presented at the EXEL conference 1993, Exeter: EXEL project.

Cudd, E.T. (1989) 'Research and report writing in the elementary grades', *The Reading Teacher*, 43 (4), pp. 268–9.

Cudd, E. and Roberts, L. (1989) 'Using writing to enhance content area learning in the primary grades', *The Reading Teacher*, 42 (6), pp. 392–404.

de Castell, S. and Luke, A. (1986) 'Models of literacy in North American schools: social and historical conditions and consequences', in S. de Castell, A. Luke and K. Egan (eds) *Literacy, Society and Schooling*, Cambridge: Cambridge University Press.

Derewianka, B. (1990) *Exploring How Texts Work*, Newtown, New South Wales: PETA.

DES (1975) *A Language for Life*, London: HMSO.

DES (1978) *Primary Education in England*, London: HMSO.

DES (1989) *Reading Policy and Practice at Age 5–14*, London: HMSO.

DES (1990) *English in the National Curriculum*, London: HMSO.

DES (1991) *Education Observed: The Implementation of the Curricular Requirements of the ERA in 1989–90*, London: HMSO.

Desforges, C. (1993) 'Subject differences in pupils' perceptions of the relevance of reading for learning', unpublished paper given at the first EXEL conference, University of Exeter.

DfE (1995) *English: a Review of Inspection Findings 1993/4*, London: HMSO.

Dillon, J.T. (1988) 'The remedial status of student questioning', *Journal of Curriculum Studies*, 20 (3), pp. 197–210.

Ebbinghaus, H. (1966) *Memory*, New York: Dover.

Fox, R. (1993) 'Teachers talking about writing at KS2', *Reading*, 27 (2), pp. 15–19.

Freebody, P. and Luke, A. (1990) 'Literacy programs: debates and demands in cultural contexts', *Prospect: Austrlian Journal of ESL*, 5 (3), pp. 99–110.

French, P. and MacLure, M. (1981) 'Teacher's questions, pupil's answers: an investigation of questions and answers in the infant classroom', *First Language*, 2 (4), pp. 31–45.

Garner, R. (1987) *Metacognition and Reading Comprehension*, Norwod, New Jersey: Ablex.

Garner, R. and Reis, R. (1981) 'Monitoring and resolving comprehension obstacles: an investigation of spontaneous text lookbacks among upper grade good and poor comprehenders', *Reading Research Quarterly*, 16, pp. 569–82.

Gilroy, A. and Moore, D. (1988) 'Reciprocal teaching of comprehension-fostering and comprehension-monitoring activities with ten primary school girls', *Educational Psychology*, 8 (1/2), pp. 41–9.

Goodman, K. (1985) 'Unity in reading', in H. Singer and R. Ruddell (eds) *Theoretical Models and Processes of Reading*, Newark, Delaware: International Reading Association.

Halliday, M. and Hasan, R. (1976) *Cohesion in English*, London: Longman.

Heath, S. B. (1983) *Ways with Words*, Cambridge: Cambridge University Press.

Hynds, J. (1993) 'A closer look at texts', in D. Wray (ed.) *Literacy: Text and Context*, Widnes: United Kingdom Reading Association.

Johnson, P. (1994) *A Book of One's Own: Developing Literacy Through Making Books*, Sevenoaks: Hodder & Stoughton.

Kerry, T. and Eggleston, J. (1988) *Topic Work in the Primary School*, London: Routledge.

Kress, G. and Knapp, P. (1992) 'Genre in a social theory of language', *English in Education*, 26 (2), pp. 4–15.

Lave, J. and Wenger, E. (1991) *Situated Learning*, Cambridge: Cambridge Univerity Press.

Lewis, D. (1992) 'Reading the range: a small-scale study of the breadth of classroom reading at KS2', *Reading*, 26 (3), pp. 12–18.

Lewis, M. and Wray, D. (1995) *Developing Children's Non-fiction Writing*, Leamington Spa: Scholastic.

Lewis, M., Wray, D. and Rospigliosi, P. (1994) 'Making reading for information more accessible to children with learning difficulties', *Support for Learning*, 9 (4), pp. 155–61.

Lewis, M., Wray, D. and Rospigliosi, P. (1995) '"No copying please!" Helping children respond to non-fiction text', *Education 3–13*, 23 (1), pp. 27–34.

Littlefair, A. (1991) *Reading All Types of Writing*, Milton Keynes: Open University Press.

Lunzer, E. and Gardner, K. (1979) *The Effective Use of Reading*, Oxford: Heinemann.

Lunzer, E. and Gardner, K. (1984) *Learning from the Written Word*, Oxford: Heinemann.

Mallett, M. (1991) *Making Facts Matter*, London: Paul Chapman.

Mandler, J. and Johnson, N. (1977) 'Remembrance of things parsed: story structure and recall', *Cognitive Psychology*, 9, pp. 111–15.

Marland, M. (ed.) (1981) *Information Skills in the Secondary Curriculum*, London: Methuen.

Martin, J. (1989) *Factual Writing: Exploring and Challenging Social Reality*, Oxford: Oxford University Press.

Martin, J.R. and Rothery, J. (1986) *Writing Project Report No.4. (1986)*, Sydney: Department of Linguistics, University of Sydney.

Medwell, J. (1993) 'A critical look at classroom contexts for writing', in D. Wray (ed.) *Literacy: Text and Context*, Widnes: United Kingdom Reading Association.

Meek, M. (1988) *How Texts Teach What Readers Learn*, Stroud: Thimble Press.

Meek, M. (1995) 'The critical challenge of the world in books for children', *Children's Literature in Education*, 26 (1), pp. 5–23.

Monk, J., Davies, P. and Karavis, S. (1992) 'Helping children access information from non-fiction books', *Books for Keeps*, 76.

Moore, P. (1988) 'Reciprocal teaching and reading comprehension: a review', *Journal of Research in Reading*, 11 (1), pp. 3–14.

Morgan, R. (1986) *Helping Children Read*, London: Methuen.

Neate, B. (1992) *Finding Out about Finding Out*, Sevenoaks: Hodder & Stoughton.

O'Brien, J. (1994a) 'Critical literacy in an early childhood classroom', *Australian Journal of Language and Literacy*, 17 (1), pp. 36–44.

O'Brien, J. (1994b) 'Show Mum you love her: taking a new look at junk mail', *Reading*, 28 (1), pp. 43–5.

OFSTED (1993) *Boys and English*, DES Ref 2/93/NS, London: HMSO.

OFSTED (1995) *English: a Review of Inspection Findings 1993/94*, London: HMSO.

Ogle, D. M. (1986) 'A teaching model that develops active reading of expository text', *The Reading Teacher*, 39 (6), pp. 564–70.

Ogle, D. M. (1989) 'The Know, Want to know, Learn strategy', in K. D. Muth (ed) *Children's Comprehension of Text*, Newark, Delaware: International Reading Association.

Olsen, M. and Gee, T. C. (1991) 'Content reading instruction in the Primary grades; perceptions and strategies', *The Reading Teacher*, 45 (4), pp. 298–306.

Palincsar, A. and Brown, A. (1984) 'Reciprocal teaching of comprehension-fostering and comprehension-monitoring activities', *Cognition and Instruction*, 1 (2), pp. 117–75.

Paris, S., Lipson, M. and Wixson, K. (1983) 'Becoming a strategic reader', *Contemporary Educational Psychology*, 8, pp. 293–316.

Poulson, L. (1992) 'Literacy and teacher assessment at Key Stage 2', *Reading*, 26 (3), pp. 6–11.

Rumelhart, D. (1980) 'Schemata: the building blocks of cognition' in R. Spiro, B. Bruce, and W. Brewer, (eds) *Theoretical Issues in Reading Comprehension*, Hillsdale, New Jersey: Lawrence Erlbaum.

Rumelhart, D. (1985) 'Toward an interactive model of reading' in H. Singer, and R. Ruddell, (eds) *Theoretical Models and Processes of Reading*, Newark, Delaware: International Reading Association.

Southgate, V., Arnold, H. and Johnson, S. (1981) *Extending Beginning Reading*, Oxford: Heinemann.

Tann, S. (1988) *Developing Topic Work in the Primary School*, London: Falmer Press.

Tizard, B. and Hughes, M. (1984) *Young Children Learning: Talking and Thinking at Home and at School*, London: Fontana.

Tizard, B., Hughes, M., Carmichael, H. and Pinkerton, G. (1983) 'Children's questions and adults answers', *Journal of Child Psychology and Psychiatry*, 24 (2), pp. 269–81.

Tonjes, M. (1988) 'Metacognitive modelling and glossing: two powerful ways to teach self responsibility', in C. Anderson (ed.) *Reading: The ABC and Beyond*, Basingstoke: Macmillan Education.

Tyack, D. and Ingram, D. (1977) 'Children's production and comprehension of questions', *Journal of Child Language*, 4 (2), pp. 211–24.

Vygotsky, L. (1962) *Thought and Language*, Cambridge, Mass.: MIT Press.

Vygotsky, L. (1978) *Mind in Society*, Cambridge, Mass.: Harvard University Press.

Waterland, L. (1985) *Read With Me*, Stroud: Thimble Press.

White, R.T. (1977) 'An overlooked objective', *Australian Science Teachers Journal*, 23 (2), pp. 124–5.

Winkworth, E. (1977) *User Education in Schools*, British Library Research and Development Department.

Winograd, P. and Bridge, C. 1986 'The comprehension of important information in written prose', in J. F. Baumann and D. E. Newark (eds) *Teaching Main Idea Comprehension*, : International Reading Association.

Woodward, C. (1992) 'Raising and answering questions in primary science: some considerations', *Evaluation and Research in Education*, 6 (2/3), pp. 145–53.

Wray, D. (1981) *Extending Reading Skills*, Lancaster: University of Lancaster.

Wray, D. (1985) *Teaching Information Skills Through Project Work*, Sevenoaks: Hodder & Stoughton.

Wray, D. (1988a) 'Literacy: the information dimension' in C. Anderson (ed.) *Reading: The ABC and Beyond*, London, Macmillan Education.

Wray, D. (1988b) *Project Teaching*, Leamington Spa: Scholastic.

Wray, D. (1991) *The Project Research Pack*, Cheltenham: Stanley Thornes.

Wray, D. (1994) *Literacy and Awareness*, Sevenoaks: Hodder & Stoughton.

Wray, D. and Lewis, M. (1992) 'Primary children's use of information books', *Reading*, 26 (3), pp. 19–24.

Wray, D. and Lewis, M. (1993) 'The reading experiences and interests of junior school children', *Children's Literature in Education*, 24 (4), pp. 251–64.

Wray, D. and Medwell, J. (1991) *Literacy and Language in the Primary Years*, London: Routledge.

Wray, D., Bloom, W. and Hall, N. (1989) *Literacy in Action*, Basingstoke: Falmer.

Index

Note: page numbers *in italics* refer to figures where these are separated from their textual reference.